CW01431417

SIMON & SCHUSTER
Rockefeller Center
1230 Avenue of the Americas
New York, NY 10020

Copyright © 1999 by Simon & Schuster Inc.
All rights reserved,
including the right of reproduction
in whole or in part in any form.

SIMON & SCHUSTER and colophon are registered
trademarks of Simon & Schuster Inc.

Designed by Amy Hill

Manufactured in the United States of America

1   3   5   7   9   10   8   6   4   2

Library of Congress Cataloging-in-Publication Data
is available.
ISBN 0-684-86480-0

The Clarion Book text stock for this book was donated by
Allan & Gray, a division of Alling & Cory,
and by Willamette Industries, in celebration of
Simon & Schuster's first seventy-five years.

Simon & Schuster

THE FIRST
SEVENTY-FIVE
YEARS

1924–1999

Contents

Foreword

DESPITE OUR TREMENDOUS GROWTH AND OUR occasional changes in management and ownership, Simon & Schuster is very much the company Richard L. Simon and M. Lincoln Schuster envisioned when they opened for business seventy-five years ago. Simon & Schuster continues to be committed to publishing good books for the general reader and remains a company whose list of titles is built with personal enthusiasm and launched with energy, style, and a sense of fun.

As we mark our seventy-fifth anniversary, we celebrate the imagination and invention of Dick Simon, Max Schuster, and Leon Shimkin, as well as the resilience and imagination of the many who have contributed to Simon & Schuster's success over the years. But most of all, we celebrate our authors, whose books have given so much pleasure to readers and made an immeasurable contribution to their lives.

Jack Romanos
PRESIDENT AND COO

BEGINNINGS

On January 2, 1924, Simon and Schuster Publishers opened for business in a small, three-room office at 37 West Fifty-seventh Street in New York City. Richard L. Simon and Max Lincoln Schuster had no employees, no authors, no manuscripts, no sales, and, it would appear, no prospects for future success. Indeed, Dick Simon and Max Schuster had their own way of doing things. Against conventional publishing wisdom, they planned to publish by first generating ideas for books and only then assigning authors to write them.

Simon and Schuster had known each other just three years before they joined forces. Simon, twenty-one years old, was selling pianos for the Aeolian Company in Manhattan, and Schuster, at twenty-four, was editing a trade magazine for an automobile association whose office was in the Aeolian Building. One day, Simon, who had been informed that Schuster liked music and might be enticed to buy a piano, dropped into

Schuster's office hoping to make a sale. Schuster wasn't interested, but the two struck up a conversation about Romain Rolland's *Jean Christophe* and became friends. Soon thereafter, Simon left the piano business and became a salesman for the publishing firm of Boni & Liveright. He and Schuster fell into the habit of lunching together and discussing plans for forming a publishing company of their own.

❧ This is the first puzzle from the first book of the first series. The answers were available on request by mail and can be found on page 159. Good luck!

HORIZONTAL

1 Pronoun
3 Albumin from castor-oil bean
7 Exist
9 Aged
11 Negative
12 Incite, hasten
13 Remote
15 Obstruction
17 Bivalves
21 Father
23 Tree
24 River in Italy
25 Owners
26 Printer's measure
27 Tree
28 Personal pronoun
29 Legislative bodies
31 Compact mass
32 Moved rapidly
34 Walk about
35 Toss
37 Small child
39 Upon
40 Small openings
41 Act

VERTICAL

1 Exclamation
2 Fairy
4 Preposition
5 Plotter
6 Pronoun
7 Express generally
8 Pronoun
10 Obstruct
12 Owns
14 Disarranged
15 Voluble talkativeness
16 Above
18 The bow of Vishnu
19 Choose
20 Assumed an attitude
22 Limb
24 Peer
29 Sorrowful
30 Rested
31 Pale
33 Incline the head
34 Move
35 Behold
36 Exist
38 Preposition

Their first project was launched when Simon heard his aunt say she wished there were a collection of crossword puzzles—a new fad—she could give to a sick friend. Simon liked the idea and persuaded the *New York Sunday World* crossword editors, F. Gregory Hartswick, Prosper Buranelli, and Margaret Petherbridge, to create the first book of puzzles. On the advice of the American News Company, which took a thousand copies of

PUZZLE No. 1   **A SOFT BEGINNING**
By GREGORIAN

THE two long central words, if solved at once, will give sufficient clues to permit of rapid solution. But should these prove elusive, surely such definitions as 9 horizontal and 29 vertical offer no difficulties. Three-letter words meaning respectively "aged" and "sorrowful" should hold few terrors for the beginner.

the book on consignment, Simon and Schuster decided to publish the puzzle book under the quickly organized Plaza Publishing imprint, so as not to be forever branded as publishers of novelty books. The puzzle book manuscript was delivered, a first printing of thirty-six hundred copies was set at a retail price of $1.35 per book (including an attached pencil), and small announcement ads were placed in the *World* and other newspapers. When publication day arrived on April 10, 1924, no one knew what to expect.

The Cross Word Puzzle Book was a raging success. Orders poured in, more than twenty clerks were hired, the office was expanded, and more books were commissioned. Each collection of puzzles sold more than 100,000 copies in the first nine months. Simon and Schuster revealed themselves to be the publishers, and the Plaza imprint was retired. Simon and Schuster made another good decision later that year by hiring seventeen-year-old Leon Shimkin as office manager.

By October 1924, "Essandess" (as they began to sign themselves) had published four books—all crossword puzzle collections, and all bestsellers. The puzzle books sold nearly one million copies and grossed $600,000 by year's end. But the puzzle book craze ended as abruptly as it began, and the staff was cut back from fifty to three: Simon, Schuster, and Shimkin. Fortunately, Simon and Schuster had acquired a few other titles during the puzzle craze. The Common Sense Library, a collection of short how-to books on money, sports, and various other topics, kept the company afloat through 1925. Then Schuster conceived a project that would reinvent the firm.

Schuster discovered a series of five-cent Little Blue Books on philosophy by Will Durant, a teacher at Columbia University, and thought that with rewriting and editing, the books, published by the small midwestern firm E. Haldeman-Julius, could be made into a single volume called *The Story of Philosophy*. The result was a substantial book, carrying the high cover price of five dollars, but Simon and Schuster backed its publication with a strong advertising campaign. When it was published on May 24, 1926, S&S had another bestseller. The book was reprinted regularly for the next three and one-half years (and is still in print today), while the

❧ Max Lincoln Schuster and Richard L. Simon turned the crossword puzzle craze into a publishing empire.

author and his wife, Ariel, embarked on a new project for the company, a series called The Story of Civilization, which began with *Our Oriental Heritage* and ended forty-eight years and eleven volumes later with *The Age of Napoleon.*

Simon and Schuster Publishers gained some respect from the publishing world with the Durant book and soon began receiving manuscripts and proposals. Several of these became bestsellers, albeit controversial ones. Four other publishers turned down Alfred Aloysius Horn and Ethelreda Lewis's *Trader Horn,* the chronicles of an implausible bum, before Simon and Schuster published the book in 1927. While many critics doubted Horn's authenticity, Dick Simon and Max Schuster vigorously promoted the book, and it became a great success. Another book, Joan Lowell's *Cradle of the Deep,* purported to be the account of Lowell's extravagant adventures aboard schooners when she was a girl. It became a 1929 bestseller but caused a sensation when the story was found to be fraudulent. Both Simon and Schuster and the Book-of-the-Month Club (which had taken the book as a selection) promised to refund the price of the book to dissatisfied customers, but no one took them up on their offer.

The Inner Sanctum

In 1930, the company moved to 386 Fourth Avenue, then New York's "Publishers' Row." Simon and Schuster each had his own office, connected by a room that housed a Ping-Pong table. During lunch, staff members often played a few games, but the table also served as a mail sorting station in the morning and a bar during publication parties. This room was the place to meet, and it soon became known as the "Inner Sanctum"—a phrase that became identified with the company.

The name "Inner Sanctum" was also used in the chatty advertising columns Simon and Schuster ran in *Publishers Weekly* and *The New York Times*. The columns invited readers with the headline, "From the Inner Sanctum of Simon and Schuster," and then proceeded to extol the virtues of Essandess books. Some of their successes at the time were *What We Live By* (1932) by Ernest Dimnet, *Van Loon's Geography* (1932) and *The Arts* (1937) by Hendrik Willem Van Loon, *How to Win Friends & Influence People* (1937) by Dale Carnegie, and *With Malice Toward Some* (1938) by Margaret Halsey.

Inner Sanctum ads would admit an occasional Essandess flop, or congratulate other publishing houses on their triumphs,

15

and sometimes would even admonish readers for ignoring a book. Occasionally, they mentioned movies and plays Max and Dick had enjoyed. These columns, which projected a distinct Essandess personality, appeared regularly from the 1930s to the 1960s, when editor in chief Jack Goodman and advertising director Nina Bourne introduced a new style of advertising.

During its earliest days, the advertising dollars Essandess spent per book were five or ten times what most other publishers spent. It was an innovation at the time to apply such marketing methods to books, but Simon and Schuster enjoyed the challenge. Schuster wrote the ads for the general public, while Simon wrote the ads for trade magazines. Everyone was expected to do everything, but, fundamentally, Schuster was the editor, Simon the salesman, and Shimkin the businessman.

Leon Shimkin,
Max Schuster, and
Dick Simon.

THE ARTS

The story of Painting and Sculpture and Architecture and Music as well as all
the so-called Minor Arts from the days of the caveman until the present time
Done into one single volume, written and illustrated by
HENDRIK WILLEM VAN LOON

❧ The dust jacket for Hendrik Willem Van Loon's
The Arts unfolded into a poster-sized map and
time line of the great events of world art.

❧ Next pages: this 1955 Inner Sanctum
ad announced the thirtieth anniversary
edition crossword puzzle book.

from THE INNER SANCTUM *of*

SIMON AND SCHUSTER, *publishers*

Rockefeller Center • *New York*

A rush of heady memories
induced by the publication of
THE TWICE-AS-BIG 30TH ANNIVERSARY EDITION
CROSSWORD PUZZLE BOOK
(The 73rd in the series!)

Thirty years ago, Your Correspondents installed themselves in a three-room office, put a sign on the door, declared themselves publishers, and went to lunch. While they were gone, a friend came to call, found nobody home and, beneath the sign

> SIMON AND SCHUSTER, PUBLISHERS

he wrote, "Of what?"*

At precisely that moment, Your Correspondents were asking this same question of each other.

Eleven days later, they had an answer. On that historic evening a lady mentioned to the Committee on New Traditions of the Inner Sanctum that she would like to send a book of crossword puzzles — a feature that appeared weekly in the New York *World*— to a friend as a birthday gift. But, to her knowledge, no such book existed.

"Why," she asked, "don't you publish a book of cross-word puzzles?"

Significant glances were exchanged all around. Investigation began before you could spell r-e-s-e-a-r-c-h. It developed that:

1. The puzzle had been running in *one* newspaper, the *World*, since December 1913.

2. As an intellectual pastime, it was highly regarded in the early 20's by members of the Algonquin set and Wit's End set — notably HEYWOOD BROUN, FRANKLIN P. ADAMS. and NEYSA MCMEIN.

3. The staff of the *World* thought that a whole book of crossword puzzles was the worst idea since Prohibition.

Your Correspondents were rocked. Nevertheless, through the good offices of F.P.A. they gained an introduction to F. GREGORY HARTSWICK, PROSPER BURANELLI, and a charming Smith College graduate named MARGARET PETHERBRIDGE — who edited the Thing in odd moments snatched from their real jobs on the *World*.

This trio spent the next two weeks rummaging through the 1500 unpublished crossword puzzles in HARTSWICK'S desk drawer. They gleaned 50.

Your Correspondents wrapped them up; sent them to the printer and, in a euphoric moment, ordered a first printing of 3,600 copies.

🚴🚴🚴 Immediately after which they were visited by intimations of fallibility. Precautionary measures were taken:

1. ESSANDESS decided to cloak their good name** (in case of disaster and disgrace) in a one-shot imprint — Plaza Publishing Company (inspired by their telephone exchange and the nearby hotel.)

2. Publication of the book was announced in an ad that measured one inch.

🚴🚴🚴 On publication day, in his *World* column, "The Conning Tower," F.P.A. jubilated:

"Hooray! Hooray! Hooray! Hooray! The Crossword Puzzle Book is out today!"

🚴🚴🚴 Within a few months, practically every newspaper in the country had acquired a daily crossword puzzle.*** By Christmas, 400,000 people had given up the Charleston for *Crossword Puzzle Books, Series 1, 2, and 3,* a brace of sharp pencils, and whatever dictionaries and encyclopedias they could find.

🚴🚴🚴 In the arenas of championship crossword puzzle tournaments, Yale was pitted against Harvard, firemen against policemen, Brooklyn against Manhattan, South against North, and brother against brother.

🚴🚴🚴 Reader, three decades and 72 collections (2.000,000 copies have been sold to date) make it plain that these puzzles are as much a part of living as coffee with breakfast and the morning newspaper.

🚴🚴🚴 It will be understood, therefore, why Your Correspondents take pride in announcing publication of the **Twice-As-Big 30th Anniversary Crossword Puzzle Book, Series 73** (Just out, $2.95.)

🚴🚴🚴 It contains 100 puzzles (instead of the usual 55)—including diagramless, story puzzles, puns and anagrams, and other surprises, the whole kit and caboodle in print for the first time.

🚴🚴🚴 It is edited, of course, by MARGARET PETHERBRIDGE FARRAR (the original MISS P., long married to publisher JOHN FARRAR) without whom no *Crossword Puzzle Book* of ours has ever appeared.

—ESSANDESS

---

* *This story has been told in print many times but is still true.*
** *Which, so far, had appeared only on the door of the office.*
*** *The New York* Times *cannot be reproached for holding out 18 years before publishing its first Sunday crossword puzzle in 1942, since the publishers themselves thought they were committed, at best, to a nine-day wonder or a permanent institution pro tem.*

Pink Slips

M. Lincoln Schuster, born in 1897, emigrated to New York from Austria as a child. He attended public schools and, at age sixteen, entered the Columbia School of Journalism. Schuster's experience as a reporter for the *World* and the United Press gave him the perfect qualifications for the publishing house he and Simon wanted to run—he excelled at generating story ideas. Schuster spent days and nights clipping and indexing stories, quotations, bits of conversation, or ideas and then filing them in an intricate system.

Each morning, Schuster stuffed his left-hand jacket pocket with 4" x 5" slips of pink, blue, and green paper. After he covered each slip with notes, he transferred it to his right-hand pocket until a pile was given to his secretary for decoding, typing, filing, and distributing. Pink slips indicated ideas that were often the seeds of book projects. Pink was also the color for "Ms" and "MQs," or maxims and maxim quotations. The blue papers held ideas for advertising copy, odd bits of fact, and references to specific books. The green slips contained reminders of people to see and things to do. All of these papers were filed under 271 classifications including Art, Civilization, Fortune, Life, Truth, the Universe, and Woman.

Schuster's elaborate system was the butt of jokes, but he explained to skeptics that this system was a way not only to create book ideas, but also to collect items for a history of wisdom on which he was working. Yet Schuster was an editor first, and his eclectic interests were a great asset. He brought to the firm many works of distinction including Will Durant's *Story of Philosophy* and the great series The History of Civilization; Thomas Craven's *A Treasury of Art Masterpieces*; and *The Bible Designed to Be Read as Living Literature,* edited by Ernest Sutherland Bates. Schuster's great commercial instincts also led him to acquire *Ripley's Believe It or Not.*

Give the Reader a Break

ichard L. Simon was born in New York City, the eldest of five children. After a childhood of writing camp songs, accompanying opera singers on the piano, and leading the glee club at Columbia College, he ended up selling pianos. Outgoing, witty, tall, handsome, and charming, Simon was a great salesman. He called on booksellers not just to sell books, but to seek their counsel. Certainly *Fortune* magazine's 1934 statement "All publishers hate all booksellers; all booksellers hate all publishers" didn't apply to Simon. Booksellers welcomed him because he knew how to sell, he would admit when he had been overly optimistic, and he wanted booksellers to be successful. Simon was the first to suggest off-pricing for books and the first to offer booksellers the privilege of returning unsold copies for credit—a practice that revolutionized the book business in 1925.

Simon always had booksellers and readers on his mind. He had bronze paperweights made for all editors. Seven inches long and two inches wide, the paperweights were embossed with Simon's motto: GIVE THE READER A BREAK. They served as a constant reminder to all of what should be most important to publishers—their readers. By his slogan, Simon meant to inspire not only editors working with authors on their texts, but the entire company, because the reader also got a break if a book had easy-to-read typefaces or the cookbooks were bound in easy-to-clean materials.

> # Give the Reader
> # a Break

Simon also contributed his energy to editorial projects by acquiring manuscripts on music, bridge, sports, and photography. Many of these books, including *Miniature Photography* (which he wrote), *A New Way to Better Golf* (the first sports instructional bestseller), and a series of song books (such as *The Rodgers and Hammerstein Song Book* and *The Cole Porter Song Book),* had long and successful lives and helped build a healthy backlist.

In the 1930s the backlist grew as well, with the development of collections and gift books, many of them appearing as "Fireside" books. *The Fireside Book of Dog Stories* was the first such title, and its success generated a number of others. There were Fireside books of love songs, American songs, chess, and a treasury of modern humor. There were even Fireside sports books. Fireside became a trademark name for Simon and Schuster and later became the name of a trade paper imprint devoted to books for family and personal improvement.

Personal improvement books have always been part of the house's publishing program. The first of these books appeared in 1925 when the then eighteen-year-old Leon Shimkin met boxing trainer Artie McGovern in his local gymnasium. Shimkin persuaded Simon to get a book out of McGovern, and the result, *The Secret of Keeping Fit,* was a strong seller.

How to Win Friends and Influence People

Hired in the company's first year during the puzzlebook craze, Leon Shimkin was the office manager, bookkeeper, and business manager. For three years, he spent his days at Simon and Schuster and his evenings at New York University's School of Commerce working on his undergraduate degree. His talent and ambition in business soon established him as the "third S" at Essandess.

Shimkin was responsible for Simon and Schuster's greatest success in the 1930s, *How to Win Friends & Influence People* by Dale Carnegie. Self-improvement was an integral part of Shimkin's personal and business philosophy, so he enrolled in a fourteen-week course of Carnegie's inspirational lectures. He was so impressed he suggested to Carnegie that he expand them into a book. Carnegie was hesitant, but Shimkin won him over. The book became the number one bestseller in 1937 and remained on the list at number six in 1938. Still in print today in every country in the world where it has been published, the book has sold more than 30 million copies.

Another of Shimkin's pet projects was J. K. Lasser's *Your Income Tax*, an annual guide that dominated the tax-book market after its first publication in 1937 for nearly half a century. On these books and many other financial and investment guides, Shimkin consulted with Sam Meyerson, a man who came to S&S as a stockroom boy in 1924 and, during sixty years with the company, became vice president and director of mail-order sales. He shared with Shimkin a talent for business.

Shimkin was soon invited to buy stock and become an equal partner with the firm's two founders. Over the next forty years, Shimkin balanced the budgets, acquired books, and created what would be a very prosperous new division of Simon and Schuster, Pocket Books.

✒ Dale Carnegie's *How to Win Friends & Influence People* has sold more than 30 million copies.

POCKET
BOOKS 1986

BRANCHING OUT

⧈

Pocket Books

| 1939 | 1943 | 1945 | 1962 | 1964 | 1977 |

n the late 1930s, the three S's teamed up with Robert Fair de Graff. Formerly of Doubleday and Blue Ribbon Books, he admired the recent success of Penguin Books in England. The four planned to create the first U.S. mass-market publisher, utilizing modern production techniques and distributing the resulting inexpensive paperback books through magazine distributors and outlets. It was the firm's intention, as de Graff said, to provide "the widest variety of books at the lowest price to the greatest number of people." The result was Pocket Books, a series of pocket-size paperback reprints of classics and recent bestsellers. Pocket set up its office in the original Inner Sanctum.

The four partners decided to test market their idea in New York City with ten titles. They acquired the books with

◦ Robert Fair de Graff with Gertrude.

terms that hardcover publishers and authors liked: a four percent royalty on the cover price and an advance of $500, to be
split evenly between author and original publisher. Artists were
commissioned to design new cover art for the paperbacks, and
the partners set a 25-cent cover price to further attract customers. At this time, Frank J. Lieberman created the bespecta-
cled kangaroo named Gertrude that would become Pocket's
logo. Shimkin set an initial printing of ten thousand copies for
each of Pocket's first ten titles: *Lost Horizon* by James Hilton,
Wake Up and Live! by Dorothea Brande, *Five Great Tragedies* by
William Shakespeare, *Topper* by Thorne Smith, *The Murder of
Roger Ackroyd* by Agatha Christie, *Enough Rope* by Dorothy
Parker, *Wuthering Heights* by Emily Brontë, *The Way of All Flesh*
by Samuel Butler, *The Bridge of San Luis Rey* by Thornton
Wilder, and *Bambi* by Felix Salten.

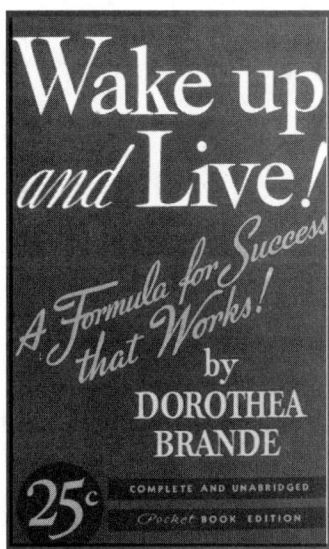

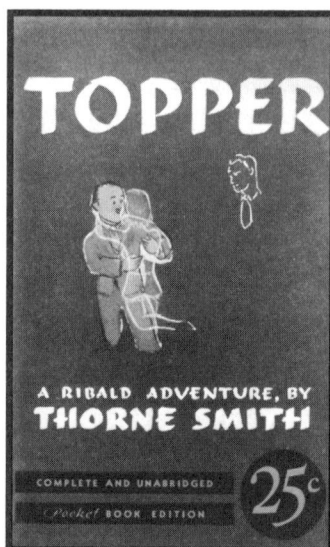

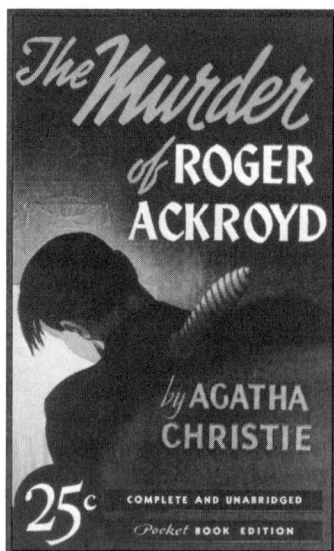

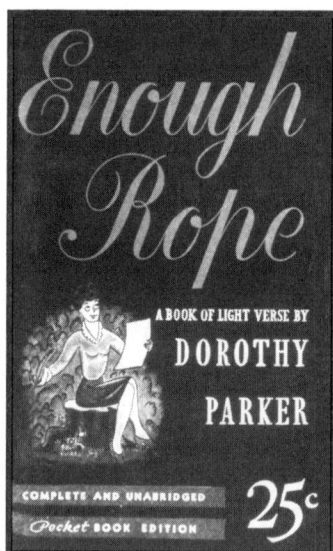

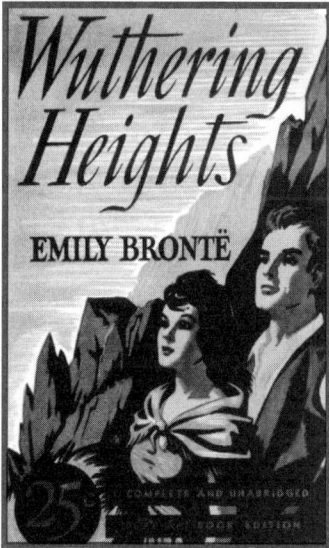

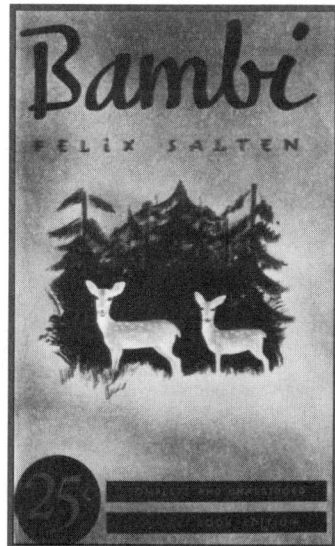

Pocket's first day of sales on June 19, 1939, must have reminded Dick Simon and Max Schuster of the puzzle-book days. The company's only telephone line was jammed with reorders from New York accounts and from out-of-state customers who had heard of the books and wanted to sell them. It wasn't long before Pocket had more than six hundred independent wholesalers across the country distributing its product through newsstands, stationery stores, grocery stores, and transportation terminals. Pocket Books was a raving success; everyone wanted paperbacks here and abroad. By 1940, Pocket Books outgrew the space provided by the Inner Sanctum and moved to 1230 Sixth Avenue in Rockefeller Center.

During the Second World War, various wartime agencies shipped 25 million Pocket Books overseas to U.S. military and government personnel. By the time Pocket published the first edition of Benjamin Spock's *Baby and Child Care* in 1946, Pocket Books titles were in every home in the country.

Having had such great success with mass distribution for Pocket Books, Simon and Schuster wondered if the same techniques could be applied to children's books. As Leon Shimkin asked at the time, "How about hitching our wagon to a stork?" Western Printing and Lithographing of Wisconsin, a company that specialized in comic books and novelty items, was persuaded to put $2 million into the creation of a new Simon and Schuster subsidiary, launched in 1943. Under the direction of George Duplaix and Albert Leventhal, Little Golden Books combined educational content for children and four-color art at 25 cents a copy. Fifty thousand copies of each title were printed, and they instantly sold out in toy stores, bookstores, and department stores. By the end of the first year, 2.7 million Golden Books had been shipped, and 2 million more were on backorder.

~❧ Marshall Field.

Enter Marshall Field

In 1944, Marshall Field, heir to the Chicago merchandising fortune, discovered Pocket Books at a newsstand in Grand Central and was so impressed with them that he mentioned to his friend Dick Simon that he was interested in building a company that would include a large book-publishing operation. Simon discussed this informal offer with Schuster, Shimkin, and de Graff. After much thought, the partners decided to sell Simon and Schuster and Pocket Books to Field for an estimated $3 million. Under the agreement, Simon and Schuster and Pocket could continue to operate with complete autonomy, providing the company with welcome financial security and the principals with long-term management contracts.

Stable and profitable years followed. Through the '40s and '50s, Simon and Schuster titles never missed the *Publishers Weekly* annual top-ten bestseller lists. With the outbreak of World War II, a number of patriotic titles hit the lists, including *Victory Through Air Power* by Alexander de Seversky, *One World* by Wendell L. Willkie, *I Never Left Home* by Bob Hope, and *General Marshall's Report* by the U.S. War Department General Staff. An inspirational book by Rabbi Joshua Liebman, *Peace of Mind*, was a top-ten bestseller in both 1947 and 1948. Some of the big best-selling novels of the post-war years were *Gentleman's Agreement* by Laura Z. Hobson in 1947, *Father of the Bride* by Edward

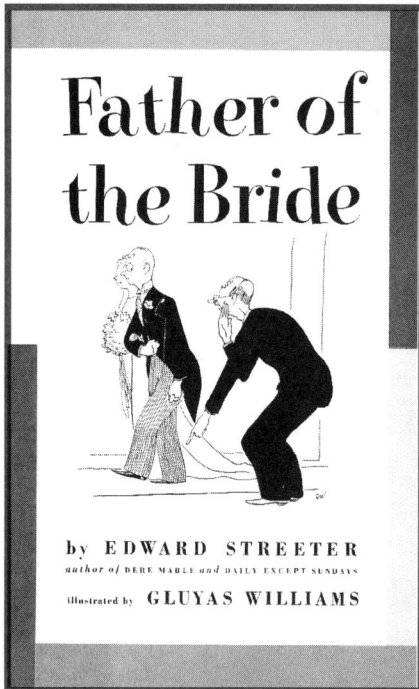

❧ *Father of the Bride,* by Edward Streeter, one of the top ten bestsellers of 1949, is republished in 1999 as Simon & Schuster Classic Edition #3.

The
Man
in
the
Gray
Flannel
Suit

a novel by

Sloan
Wilson

~ Sloan Wilson
also wrote the
1958 bestseller
A Summer Place.

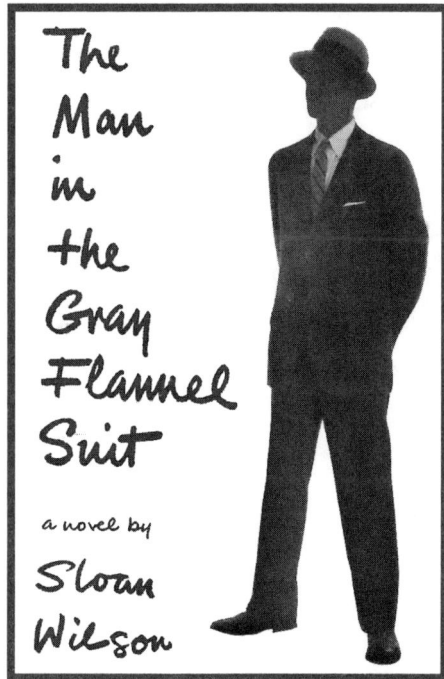

Streeter in 1949, *The Cardinal* by Henry Morton Robinson in 1950, *Zorba the Greek* by Nikos Kazantzakis in 1953, and *The Man in the Gray Flannel Suit* by Sloan Wilson in 1955. Distinguished nonfiction came to the list from authors like Bertrand Russell (*A History of Western Philosophy*), Edward R. Murrow (*This I Believe*), Robert Oppenheimer (*Science and the Common Understanding*), and William H. Whyte (*The Organization Man*).

In this period, the company published some of the best music and cartoon books on the market. There were the famous songbooks that Dick Simon acquired, as well as the best-selling *Fireside Book of Folk Songs*. In fact, music books were so

35

much a part of the publishing program that there was a piano in the editor in chief's office that copy editors used to check manuscripts. In the '50s and '60s, cartoon and humor books by the likes of Walt Kelly; Charles Addams; James Thurber; Whitney Darrow, Jr.; the lovable Sam Levenson; and the irascible S. J. Perelman graced the list. And Kay Thompson's wonderful *Eloise*, the story of the New York Plaza Hotel's enfant terrible, became both a bestseller and an instant classic.

Simon, Schuster, and Shimkin Redux

Marshall Field's death in 1957 threw the company's future into question. Field had designated in his will that the ownership of Simon and Schuster and Pocket was to pass to a nonprofit foundation. Shimkin disliked the idea and negotiated with the Field trustees. The three S's bought back Simon and Schuster. Shimkin, together with James M. Jacobson, acquired Pocket Books.

Simon, Schuster, and Shimkin also made a pact for the future ownership of their company that allowed the remaining two partners to buy out the stock if one partner were to leave the company. Dick Simon, who had been having health problems, retired later that year, leaving Schuster and Shimkin as equal partners. Schuster stayed on as president until he retired in 1966.

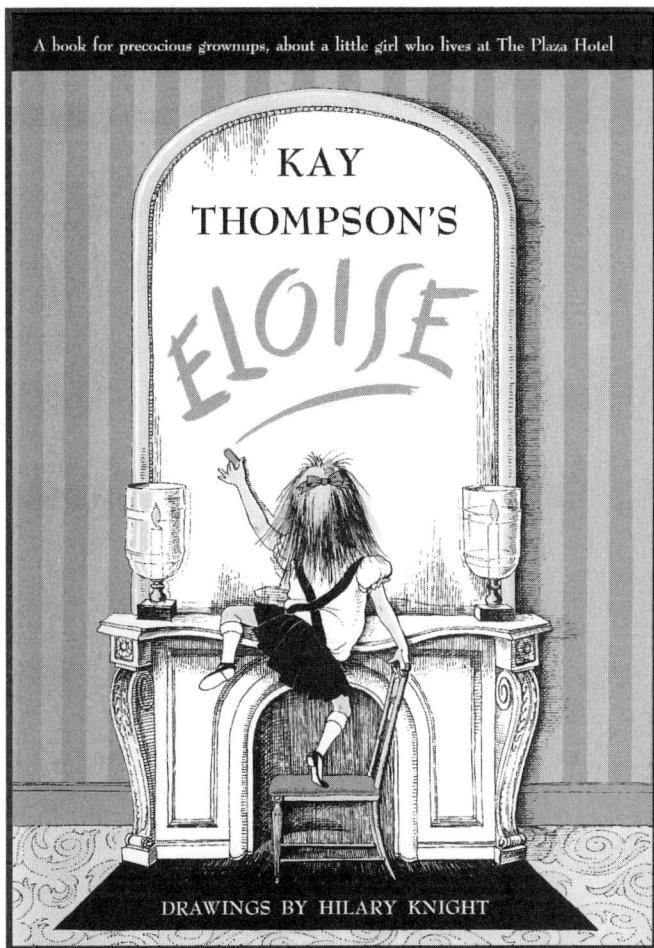

A book for precocious grownups, about a little girl who lives at The Plaza Hotel

KAY
THOMPSON'S
ELOISE

DRAWINGS BY HILARY KNIGHT

❧ The irrepressible Eloise, created by Kay Thompson.

Upon Schuster's retirement, Shimkin negotiated a series of transactions with Schuster's stock and Pocket Books' stock, allowing for the consolidation of the two companies into Simon & Schuster, Inc. At the time of the merger, Shimkin compared the restructured company to a block of brownstones interrelated for general services, such as finance, production, and distribution, but creatively autonomous.

CHANGES

During the late '50s and early '60s, even before Schuster retired, there were major changes in management and company structure. Jack Goodman, who had been both editor in chief and head of advertising, died suddenly in 1957; Dick Simon retired; Albert Leventhal resigned. Peter Schwed, who had long been both subsidiary rights manager and a key editor, became publisher of Simon & Schuster. A new generation was emerging. Robert Gottlieb, who arrived in 1955 as an assistant, was a charismatic young editor who brought a new perspective and range to the S&S list. With his great enthusiasm, Gottlieb challenged the company to publish books that were fresh, controversial, and occasionally a bit shocking. With Max Schuster's blessing, Peter Schwed chose Gottlieb to head the editorial department in 1959.

Gottlieb brought many writers to S&S including Doris Lessing, Jessica Mitford, Charles Portis, Robert Crichton, Edna O'Brien, Bruce Jay Friedman, and Chaim Potok. Perhaps

   🌺 Robert Gottlieb.

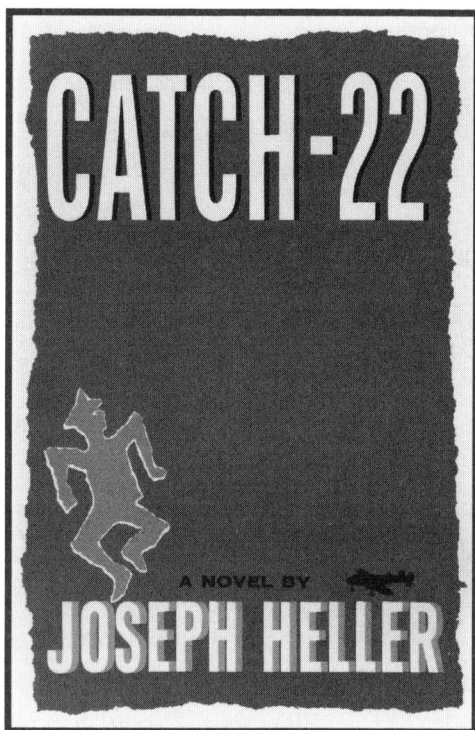

🌺 Thirty-three
years after the
publication of
Catch-22, Heller
wrote the sequel,
Closing Time.

the most celebrated of his acquisitions was Joseph Heller's *Catch-22*, which Gottlieb launched in 1961. Although *Catch-22* did not initially make the national bestseller lists (it did hit the lists in 1970 when the film was released), this classic satire of the insanity of war has stayed in print in numerous editions.

Gottlieb's colleagues were Nina Bourne, who succeeded Jack Goodman as head of advertising, and Tony Schulte who succeeded Leventhal as sales director. Under this triumverate, S&S editors continued to produce books that won awards and hit the bestseller lists. Joseph Barnes, a longtime editor of nonfiction, who had helped Wendell Willkie write *One World,* edited many distinguished books. His dedication was such that he worked with William Shirer on *The Rise and Fall of the Third Reich* for six months to the exclusion of all other projects. Their concentrated efforts were rewarded when the book won the 1961 National Book Award. In 1967, Justin Kaplan's *Mr. Clemens and Mark Twain,* also edited by Joe Barnes, won both the Pulitzer Prize and the National Book Award. Will and Ariel Durant, who had been with S&S since the early days and were now edited by Michael Korda, won a 1968 Pulitzer Prize for *Rousseau and Revolution* (vol. 10 in The Story of Civilization). Bob Gottlieb edited Jessica Mitford's *The American Way of Death* (1963); Tony Schulte edited Larry Collins and Dominique Lapierre's *Is Paris Burning?* (1965); Gottlieb hit the bestseller lists with Robert Crichton's *The Secret of Santa Vittoria* (1966) and three novels by Harold Robbins—*The Carpetbaggers* (1961), *Where Love Has Gone* (1962), and *The Adventurers* (1966); Korda edited seven Irving Wallace novels that dominated the bestseller lists between 1960 and 1969.

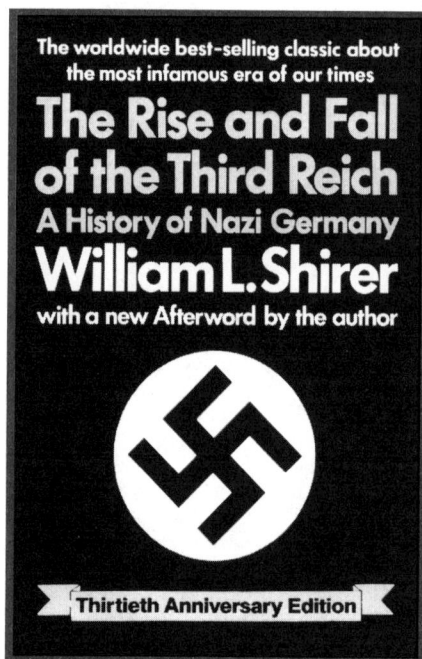

❧ *The Rise and Fall of the Third Reich* by William L. Shirer, winner of the 1961 National Book Award, was reissued in a thirtieth-anniversary edition in 1990.

The 1969 publication of *The Love Machine* by Jacqueline Susann marked a turning point in how commercial books were promoted and sold. Jackie Susann and her husband, Irving Mansfield, were experts at a kind of show-business publicity that had never been used in book publishing. S&S learned quickly from the Mansfields, and modern book marketing was born.

In 1968, the company experienced another changing of the guard, when Gottlieb left S&S to become president and editor in chief of Knopf—taking Schulte, Bourne, and a number of authors with him. Peter Schwed was faced once again with rebuilding the team. The editorial helm of S&S was given to another young man, Michael Korda.

Michael Korda had joined S&S in 1958. First assigned to read and edit manuscripts for Dick Simon's brother Henry, he later worked under Schuster. But Korda soon allied himself with what he called "Gottlieb's camp," where young editors could challenge the old ways and flourish. Flourish he did. Over the years, Korda has edited books by Carlos Castaneda, Cher, Mary Higgins Clark, Jackie Collins, Joan Didion, Graham Greene, Justin Kaplan, Henry Kissinger, David McCullough, Larry McMurtry, Presidents Nixon and Reagan, and Richard Rhodes. In his thirty years as editor in chief, Korda has acquired and edited more than one hundred *New York Times* bestsellers.

∽ Michael Korda.

Three years after Korda's arrival, another young man joined the company, someone who would eventually become the "fourth S" in S&S history. Richard E. Snyder began his career at S&S in 1961 as a salesman for Pocket Books. He quickly rose in the company, displaying both editorial vision and business expertise. In 1968, after Gottlieb, Schulte, and Bourne departed, Schwed made Snyder his associate publisher, and in 1970, when Schwed announced that he was "kicking [himself] upstairs," Snyder became publisher of S&S Trade with Schwed's blessing.

S&S had long been known as a publisher of excellent nonfiction, but a new kind of nonfiction success, and an important moment for the company, came in 1974 when Snyder acquired *All the President's Men* by Bob Woodward and Carl Bernstein. He and editor Alice Mayhew, whose expertise as an editor of nonfiction was to become legendary, shaped a book and publishing plan that produced not only an instant bestseller but an important record of a central moment in American history. In a record-breaking auction held by director of subsidiary rights Millie Marmur, *All the President's Men* brought in the first seven-figure price for nonfiction paperback rights.

All the President's Men was a great victory for Snyder, the company, and especially Mayhew. She had arrived at S&S in 1971 and was essential to continuing S&S's reputation as a premier nonfiction publisher. Editorial director of S&S since 1986, she has gathered an impressive list of authors, including Stephen Ambrose, Michael Beschloss, Taylor Branch, Frances FitzGerald, Doris Kearns Goodwin, Walter Isaacson, J. Anthony Lukas, William Shawcross, James B. Stewart, and Garry Wills.

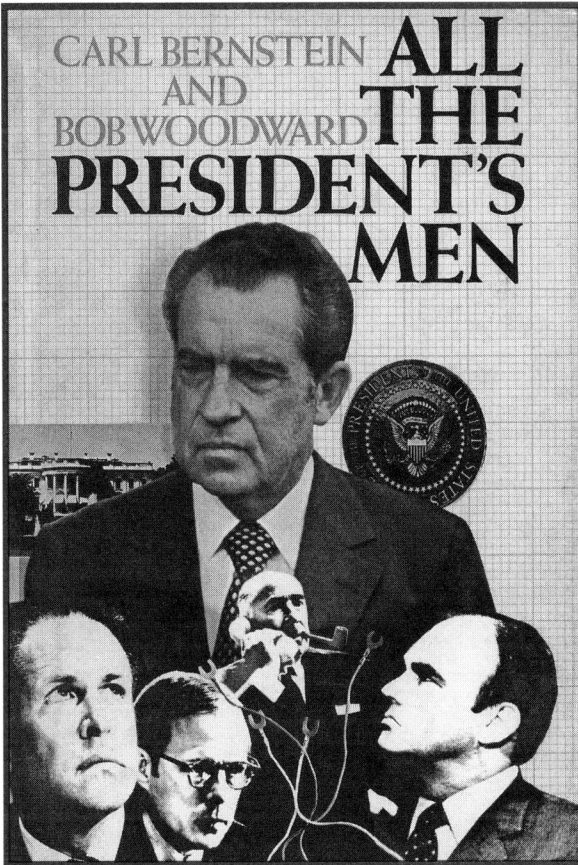

∾ *All the President's Men,* by Carl Bernstein and Bob
Woodward, is republished in 1999, on the twenty-
fifth anniversary of its original publication, as
Simon & Schuster Classic Edition #1.

During the '70s and early '80s, S&S published bestselling books that would become trendsetters. *Looking for Mr. Goodbar* by Judith Rossner illuminated the dark dangers of the singles' scene. *Our Bodies, Our Selves* by The Boston Women's Health Book Collective and *Against Our Will* by Susan Brownmiller gave voice and direction to the women's movement. *Pumping Iron* by Charles Gaines and George Butler introduced readers to Arnold Schwarzenegger and the world of competitive bodybuilding. The bodybuilding and fitness trend was further fueled by *Arnold: The Education of a Bodybuilder* by Arnold Schwarzenegger and *Jane Fonda's Workout Book* by Jane Fonda. Woodward and Bernstein continued writing the Watergate story in *The Final Days*. Mary Higgins Clark, whose first S&S novel, *Where Are the Children?*, had been a paperback bestseller, hit the hardcover lists with her second novel, *A Stranger Is Watching.* James B. Stewart's

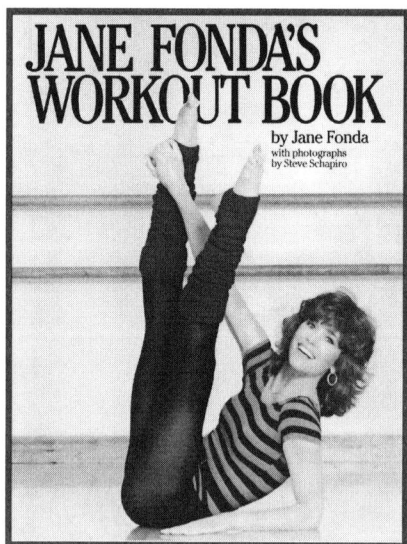

⤳ *Jane Fonda's Workout Book,* a major bestseller, launched the 1980s women's fitness trend.

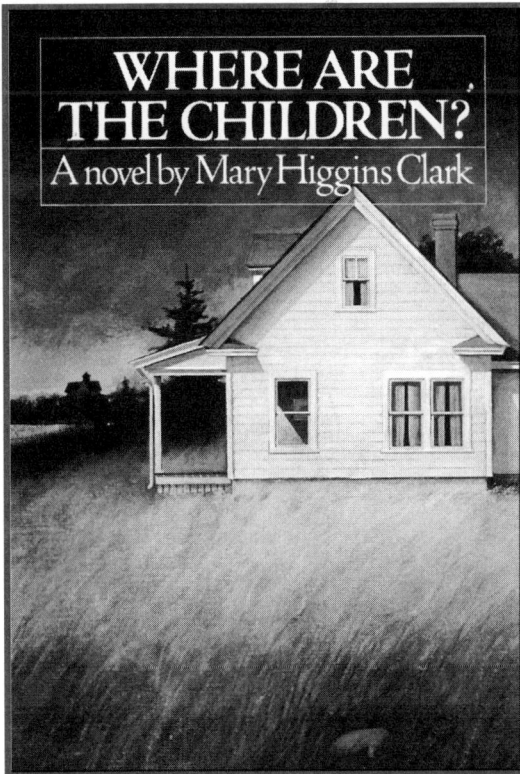

↙ Mary Higgins Clark's first mystery, *Where Are the Children?*, is republished in 1999 as Simon & Schuster Classic Edition #2.

first book, *The Partners*, was a bestseller, and Robert Allen's *Nothing Down* launched a renewed trend in personal finance books.

S&S books also continued to win prizes. David McCullough won the National Book Award in 1978 for *The Path Between the Seas* and again in 1982 for *Mornings on Horseback.* Justin Kaplan won his second National Book Award in 1981 for *Walt Whitman.*

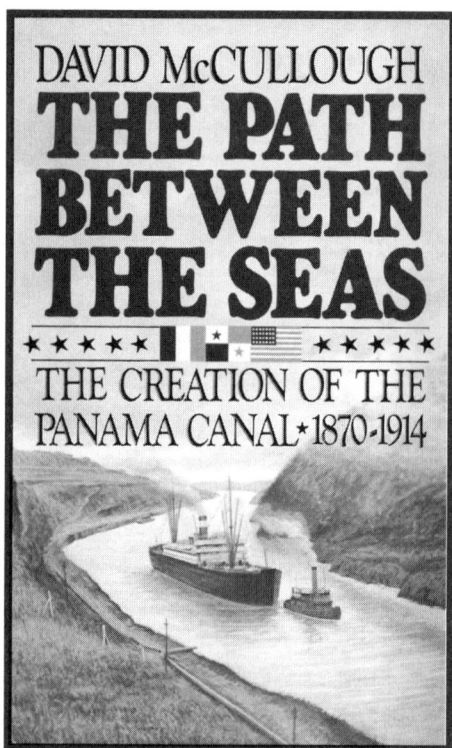

❧ *The Path Between the Seas*
by David McCullough.

~ Richard Snyder.

The eighties were years of corporate restructuring, internal expansion, acquisition, and management changes. Dick Snyder was now fully occupied by a rapidly expanding corporation, and the Simon & Schuster Trade Division had its own management teams. In 1980, Dan Green was named publisher, and in 1984 he became president, with David Cully as publisher. In 1985, Jack Romanos joined S&S as president of the trade division and the mass market division, which then included Pocket Books and the Children's and Audio publishing units. When Dan Green resigned in 1986, Romanos appointed as president Joni Evans, who had come to S&S in 1974 first as director of subsidiary rights and later publisher of her own imprint. Romanos also appointed Charles Hayward as publisher.

The Simon & Schuster hardcover imprint continued to publish award winners and bestsellers. Larry McMurtry won the Pulitzer Prize for *Lonesome Dove* in 1986. Two years later, Richard Rhodes won the Pulitzer Prize, the National

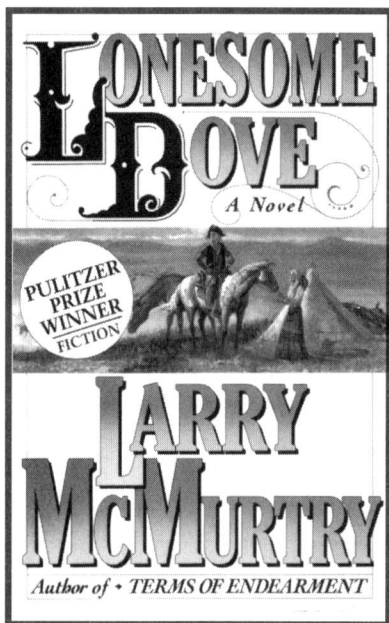

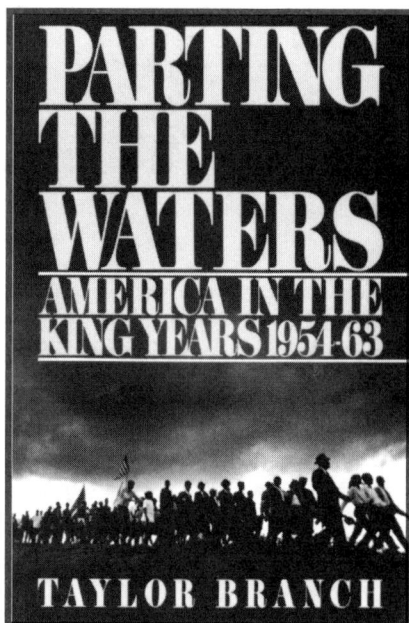

~ Pulitzer Prize winners *Lonesome Dove* by Larry McMurtry and *Parting the Waters* by Taylor Branch.

Book Award, and the National Book Critics Circle Award for *The Making of the Atomic Bomb,* and Taylor Branch received the Pulitzer Prize for *Parting the Waters* in 1989. Daniel Yergin won the Pulitzer Prize for *The Prize* in 1992, and in 1993, Simon & Schuster claimed two Pulitzers: for Garry Wills's *Lincoln at Gettysburg* and David McCullough's *Truman.* In 1995, Doris Kearns Goodwin won the Pulitzer Prize for *No Ordinary Time,* making it the seventh S&S title to win a Pulitzer in nine years.

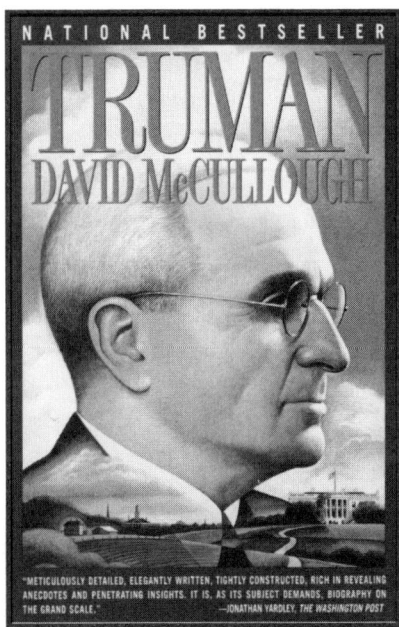

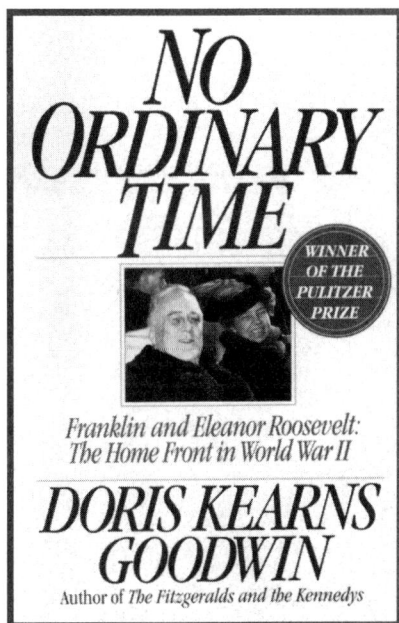

~ More Pulitzer Prize winners: *Truman* by David McCullough and *No Ordinary Time* by Doris Kearns Goodwin.

From the mid-'80s and into the '90s, S&S continued to stake a claim on the fiction bestseller lists with *Less Than Zero* by Bret Easton Ellis in 1985, *Postcards from the Edge* by Carrie Fisher in 1987, and *Streets of Laredo* by Larry McMurtry in 1993, as well as books by Carlos Castaneda, Mary Higgins Clark, Jackie Collins, Shirley Conran, Harold Coyle, Clive Cussler, Barbara Delinsky, Richard Paul Evans, and Sally Quinn. There were nonfiction bestsellers such as Allan Bloom's *The Closing of the American Mind* (1987), David Hackworth's *About Face* (1989), James B. Stewart's *Den of Thieves* (1991), Betty Friedan's *The Fountain of Age* (1993), Henry Kissinger's *Diplomacy* (1994), William J. Bennett's *The Book of Virtues* (1994), David Herbert Donald's *Lincoln* (1995), Hillary Rodham Clinton's *It Takes a Village* (1996), and Stephen Ambrose's *Undaunted Courage* (1996).

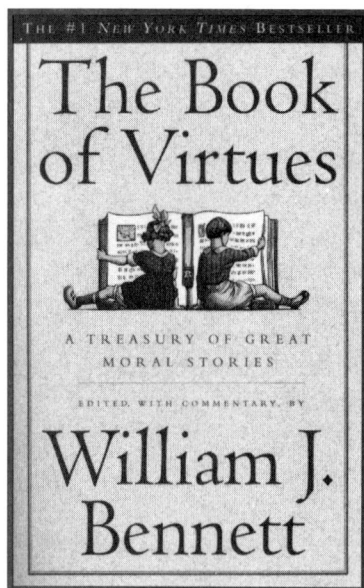

THE #1 NEW YORK TIMES BESTSELLER

The Book of Virtues

A TREASURY OF GREAT
MORAL STORIES

EDITED, WITH COMMENTARY, BY

William J. Bennett

~ *The Book of Virtues* by William J. Bennett is one of the company's biggest bestsellers, with over 2.5 million copies in print.

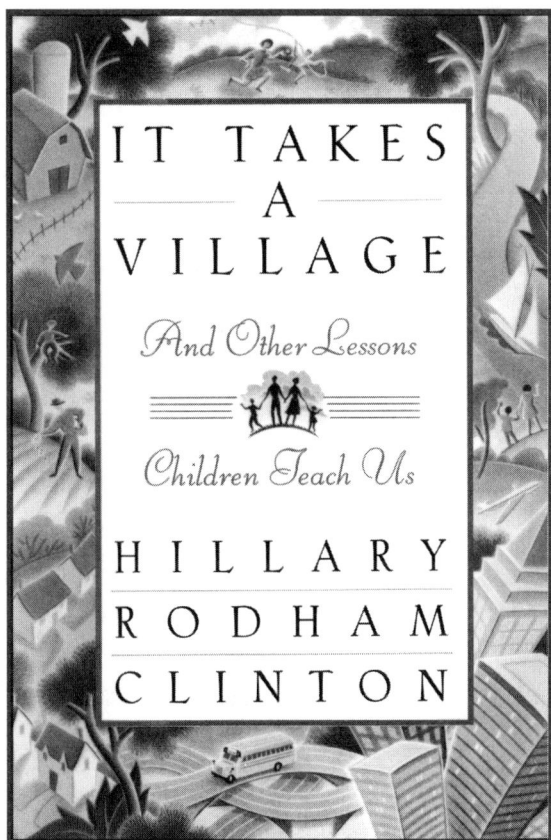

> ❧ *It Takes a Village,* by Hillary Rodham Clinton,
> was a *New York Times* bestseller for twenty
> weeks.

There were also notable books by Ben Bradlee, William Greider, Richard Nixon, Ronald Reagan, Mary Matalin and James Carville, Walter Isaacson, Evan Thomas, Ann Rule, The Duchess of York, and Howard Stern.

Longtime editors Fred Hills and Robert Bender also brought in some of the biggest bestsellers of the times and continue to do so today. In addition to his work with Pulitzer Prize–winner Dan Yergin and number-one fitness author Jane Fonda, Hills has acquired such works as *The Great Depression of 1990* by Ravi Batra, *The Different Drum* by M. Scott Peck, and *Wealth Without Risk* by Charles J. Givens. Bender has had success with *Capote* by Gerald Clarke, *It's Always Something* by Gilda Radner, and *Beating the Street* by Peter Lynch.

Since the earliest days of The Common Sense Library, S&S has combined editorial vision and marketing innovation to become the leader in publishing a wide variety of self-help books—financial, health and fitness, sports-and books to motivate and inspire. S&S has dominated bestseller lists with such personal finance books as *Strategic Investing* by Douglas R. Casey, *Creating Wealth* by Robert Allen, and *Making the Most of Your Money* by Jane Bryant Quinn, as well as books by The Motley Fool (Tom and David Gardner), and recent books by Harry Dent and David Dreman.

Ever since Artie McGovern's *The Secret of Keeping Fit*, books in the health and fitness category have regularly appeared on S&S lists not only with titles from Schwarzenegger and Fonda but with *Total Fitness in 30 Minutes a Week*, *Running and Being*, *The Body Principal,* and *The New Pritikin Program.* From the early *A New Way to Better Golf* to *Harvey Penick's*

Little Red Book, which has sold over two million copies, sports books have been a successful part of the S&S list.

Books of inspiration and motivation have also appeared regularly from S&S. Robert Asahina, an editor with the company from 1983 to 1996, acquired Stephen Covey's *The 7 Habits of Highly Effective People,* Anthony Robbins's *Unlimited Power,* and Susan Powter's *Stop the Insanity.* Recently S&S has launched several highly successful books by Iyanla Vanzant: *In the Meantime, The Value in the Valley, Acts of Faith,* and *One Day My Soul Just Opened Up.*

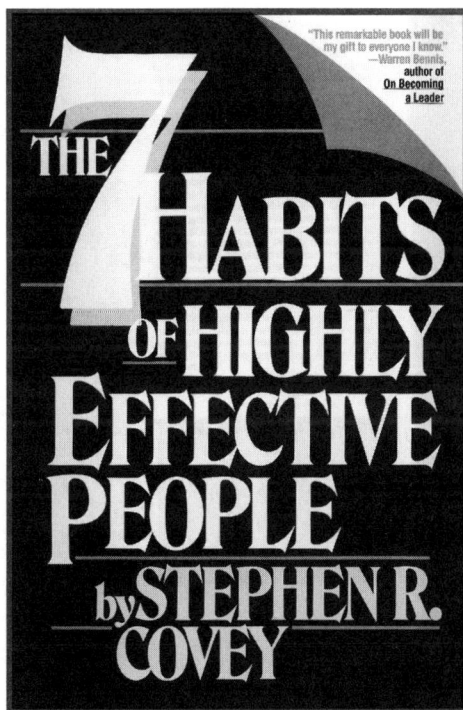

❧ The trade paperback edition of *The Seven Habits of Highly Effective People,* by Stephen R. Covey, has been on the *New York Times* bestseller list for 272 weeks.

Deluxe Trade Paperback Edition

THE *NEW YORK TIMES* BESTSELLER

THE

ROAD LESS
TRAVELED

A New
Psychology of Love,
Traditional Values and
Spiritual Growth

OVER 6
MILLION
COPIES IN
PRINT!

M. SCOTT PECK, M.D.

Author of *The Road Less Traveled and Beyond*

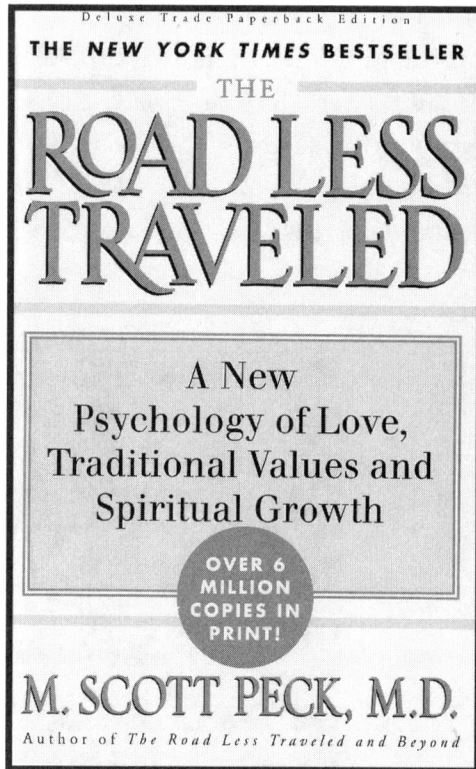

The Road Less Traveled was on the *New York Times* bestseller list for ten years.

GROWTH FROM WITHIN

◪

As the S&S imprint was growing and prospering during the last three decades, so were both the Trade division and the company at large.

In 1975, Leon Shimkin sold Simon & Schuster, Inc., to Gulf + Western and retired. G+W's chairman, Charles Bluhdorn, was anxious to acquire a major publishing house that could collaborate with Paramount Pictures, and he identified Snyder as the man who could take S&S in the right direction. When G+W bought the company, Snyder became president of Simon & Schuster, Inc.

New Imprints

Fueled by the conviction that S&S could be bigger and better, Snyder began the process that would eventually take the company from a medium-sized

New York trade publisher to a global multimedia publisher.

From 1976 to 1982, existing imprints were expanded and new ones added so that what had been singularly S&S soon became the Simon & Schuster Trade Division, a group of editorially independent publishing units. In 1977, James H. Silberman, who had been editor in chief of Random House, was persuaded to head up his own imprint, Summit Books, under the S&S umbrella. Summit's first book, *The Women's Room* by Marilyn French, became an international bestseller. Among the notable and bestselling titles on Summit's list were *The Man Who Mistook His Wife for a Hat* by Oliver Sacks, *The Price of Power* by Seymour M. Hersh, *The Great Shark Hunt* by Hunter S. Thompson, *The Cinderella Complex* by Collette Dowling, *The Kennedys* by Peter Collier and David Horowitz, and *No Bad Dogs* by Barbara Woodhouse.

Kenan Books, created shortly after Summit, was to be an imprint headed up by Dan Green, who had served first as publicity and then marketing director of S&S for years, but Kenan had barely published its first book when Snyder moved Green to S&S as publisher in 1980.

Wyndham books under Larry Freundlich was short-lived but did publish the 1980 bestseller *Green Monday* by Michael M. Thomas.

In 1979, Joni Evans was given her own imprint, Linden Press, which prospered by publishing authors like Dr. Isadore Rosenfeld, Jeffrey Archer, Helen Gurley Brown, Michael Korda, and Mario Puzo. Following Dan Green's departure in 1986, however, Linden too ceased to publish, as Evans became president of the trade division.

Another imprint, Poseidon, which had been a Pocket Books imprint under Ann Patty, became an imprint of the S&S Trade Division in the early '90s.

Simon & Schuster Trade Paperbacks

In 1970, S&S began publishing selected titles in trade paperback format to meet changing consumer demand. Two imprints, Fireside and Touchstone, were established to provide formats for books that Simon & Schuster believed would find a broader audience in paperback but were not appropriate for mass-market distribution. At first, the Fireside and Touchstone publishing programs were ad hoc affairs; books were reissued in one imprint or the other, and books from other publishers were bought for reprint at an uneven pace with little thought of how to market the books. This changed in 1986 when the trade paperbacks were separated from S&S hardcover and established as a freestanding unit within the Simon & Schuster Trade Division with its own publisher, editorial, and publicity departments.

Today, the Fireside imprint is reserved for practical books on subjects such as self-help, parenting and childcare, popular psychology, health, and medicine. The list includes how-to titles on just about any topic including games, sports, cooking, gardening, finding a job, and running a business. Among the bestselling authors published by this imprint are Stephen Covey, Susan Powter, Anthony Robbins, and Iyanla Vanzant. The Touchstone imprint publishes works of serious nonfiction in the areas of current affairs, history, biography, women's studies, science, economics, and philosophy. Its list includes works by Stephen Ambrose, Doris Kearns Goodwin, Viktor E. Frankl, David McCullough, M. Scott Peck, Bertrand Russell, James B. Stewart, and Colin Turnbull.

In January 1995, a new trade paperback imprint was launched, Scribner Paperback Fiction. Combining classics of American fiction from the extraordinary backlists of Charles Scribner's Sons and Simon & Schuster with reprints of contemporary fiction, SPF publishes classic novels by such writers as Edith Wharton, F. Scott Fitzgerald, Langston Hughes, and Ernest Hemingway, as well as contemporary novels by such writers as Don DeLillo, Jack Finney, Mary Gaitskill, Ursula Hegi, Andrei Makine, Josephine Tey, Reynolds Price, Ishmael Reed, and Robert Stone.

In the spring of 1995, S&S Trade Paperbacks launched S&S Libros en Espanol. Books on health, fitness, child care, self-help, and inspiration are available in Spanish, often at the same time they are published in English.

Under publisher Mark Gompertz, associate publisher Chris Lloreda, and editor in chief Trish Todd, trade paperbacks are a highly successful division of S&S, publishing both reprints from hardcover publishers and trade paperback original titles. In fact, S&S trade paperbacks now have sales over $100 million per year, more than triple its sales since 1986.

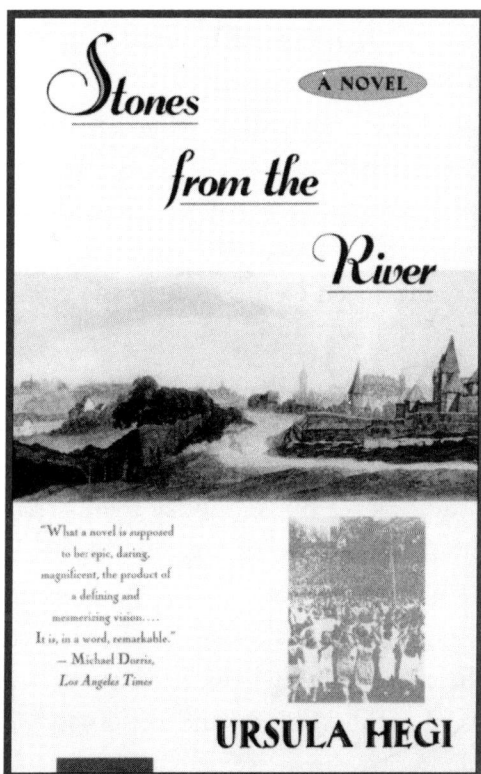

Stones from the River by Ursula Hegi.

The Expansion of Pocket Books

As other parts of the company were growing and expanding, so too was Pocket Books. Pocket's history reflects changing public taste, and its imprints have always been created or adjusted in response to the expressed needs of readers.

By the late 1940s, Pocket Books, and paperbacks in general, had become a standard fixture of popular culture. Pocket wanted to offer a greater variety of titles, however, so new imprints were established to expand Pocket's offerings. In 1948, Pocket introduced Comet Books, a line of inexpensive books for ten through sixteen year olds. Reprints of titles by fine contemporary writers, Comet Books were illustrated in two colors. In the '60s, Lantern Press was established to publish thematic short-story anthologies. As consumer tastes changed, so did Pocket Books. Today there are two juvenile paperback imprints: Minstrel Books, which publishes books for readers under age twelve, and Archway Paperbacks, whose books are for readers twelve and older. These imprints publish such successful writers as R. L. Stine, Bruce Coville, Christopher Pike, Bill Wallace, and Peg Kehret. The young-adult publishing program also includes lines of books based on the popular programs *Sabrina, the Teenage Witch,* and *Clueless.* In addition, there are series based on *Buffy the Vampire Slayer* and *Full House.*

Though Pocket has had success with several adult imprints, none has been so enduring as Washington Square Press, which is celebrating its fortieth anniversary. Acquired in 1959 from New York University Press, Washington Square Press originally published text and reference books. In the '60s and '70s, WSP offered literary classics and backlist titles. Since the '80s, WSP has been one of the leading paperback publishers of fine contemporary literature and has published such titles as *The Color Purple* by Alice Walker, *Montana 1948* by Larry Watson, *Kitchen* by Banana Yoshimoto, *Cowboys Are My Weakness* by Pamela Huston, and *Perfume* by Patrick Suskind.

In 1979, Pocket launched the *Star Trek* series. The *Star Trek* television program was originally broadcast from 1967 to 1969 and has remained tremendously popular in syndication. The *Star Trek* novels, based on the further adventures of the television characters, became a phenomenon by the mid-1980s, and in 1988 Pocket published its first *Star Trek* hardcover, *Spock's World*, a *New York Times* bestseller. With continued publication of titles based on the original *Star Trek* characters, as well as titles based on the newer TV series *Star Trek: The Next Generation, Deep Space Nine, Voyager* and various Paramount movies, *Star Trek* has become a tremendously successful franchise.

Pocket expanded into hardcover publication in 1988 and since then has published many bestselling novels by Judith McNaught, Julie Garwood, and Jude Deveraux, as well as such bestsellers as *She's Come Undone* by Wally Lamb, *See, I Told You So* by Rush Limbaugh, *Star Trek Generation* by J. M. Dillard, *Tears of Rage* by John Walsh and Susan Schindenette, and *I Can't Believe I Said That* by Kathie Lee Gifford.

A new imprint, MTV Books, was added as a result of a joint publishing venture with MTV. In addition to publishing bestselling titles based on such popular programs as *The Real World, Road Rules,* and *Beavis and Butt-head,* the imprint also publishes original works. The MTV Books fiction program, a line of original trade paperback fiction by young American authors, was launched in fall 1998.

Over the last sixty years, Pocket's mass-market reprint business has remained strong. Today it publishes such best-selling authors as V. C. Andrews, Mary Higgins Clark, Clive Cussler, and Ann Rule.

In every one of the last eight years but one, including 1998, Pocket Books had more *New York Times* paperback best-sellers than any other publisher.

NEW DIVISIONS

Children's Publishing

S&S sold its share in Golden Books to Western Publishing in 1958, and reintroduced a children's picture-book publishing program in the sixties that lasted for several years. In 1984, to expand the company further, a new children's division was created. S&S launched three imprints: Little Simon, a line of sturdy picture books for very young children; Wanderer, a line of books for 8 to 12 year olds that was enhanced by the acquisition of the Nancy Drew and the Hardy Boys franchises; and Windmill Books, founded by Robert Kraus.

S&S Children's Publishing grew dramatically with the 1994 acquisition of Macmillan and the integration of its superb children's imprints and rich backlist. The S&S Children's Publishing division joined the ranks of the largest publishers of children's books in the U.S. Under the current leadership of Rick Richter, S&S is a dynamic and innovative publisher of children's books in a variety of formats and under a number of distinctive and distinguished imprints that publish for ages ranging from pre-school to young adult: Aladdin Paperbacks, Simon & Schuster Books for Young Readers, Margaret K. McElderry Books, Atheneum Books for Young Readers, Little Simon, and Simon Spotlight. The Children's Publishing division has added to the value of Viacom's brands with *Rug Rats* and *Blue's Clues*.

New Media

In 1986, Simon & Schuster Audio was launched. It was begun as both an audio and video unit, but the company soon realized that the market was too limited to support the development of original video product. The audio market, however, began to open and grow as inexpensive, portable tape players became omnipresent. S&S took advantage of the market potential by releasing audiobooks simultaneously with new hardcover releases and merchandising its audiobooks aggressively in stores. Today, S&S is the world's second largest audio publisher. Seth Gershel, who began with S&S Audio as director of audio sales and is currently its publisher, credits the success of this division to its structure as a freestanding and independent unit—another "brownstone" in Leon Shimkin's original vision for the company.

Today, S&S Audio has a backlist of more than 800 audiobooks and publishes 120 new titles each year, many of which are read by the book's author. Among its most successful audiobooks are David McCullough's *Truman*, Caleb Carr's *The Alienist*, Richard Herrnstein and Charles Murray's *The Bell Curve*, Doris Kearns Goodwin's *No Ordinary Time*, Judy Blume's *Summer Sisters*, Tom Clancy's *Clear and Present Danger*, Don DeLillo's *Underworld*, Winston Groom's *Forrest Gump*, and Charles Kuralt's *American Moments*. S&S has sold well over one million copies of Stephen Covey's *The 7 Habits of Highly Effective People*. S&S has also received Grammy awards for audiobooks written and read by Gilda Radner, George Burns, and Hillary Rodham Clinton.

In 1994, S&S Interactive was created to produce original CD-ROMs—a new medium. S&S Interactive, currently headed by Gilles Dana, creates exciting new products each year, such as *Douglas Adams Starship Titanic* and *The Joy of Cooking*.

Online

On January 2, 1996 (exactly seventy-two years to the day since Dick Simon and Max Schuster opened their first office), S&S Online, under publisher Lisa Mandel, was formed to explore the new opportunities of online technology. When the company Web site SimonSays.com was launched in June of 1996, it quickly became an essential part of S&S's ever-evolving efforts to be in the forefront of modern marketing techniques. This group showcases and promotes authors and books as well as providing support for the new online retailers.

International

With the acquisition of Prentice-Hall in 1984, Simon & Schuster gained a major foothold in international educational publishing. In 1986, international operations were expanded with the establishment of consumer publishing units in the United Kingdom and Australia.

S&S UK and S&S Australia were at first beachheads in the world's second-largest English-language market, but in the last several years, both units have built lively original publishing programs as well as publishing group-owned titles. S&S UK, under publishing director Nick Webb, and S&S Australia, under publishing director Jon Attenborough, have not only become the publishers of a number of S&S titles but also provided a gateway into many world markets.

Nearly fifty percent of both units' titles originate with S&S in New York, and they are the publishers of Mary Higgins Clark, V. C. Andrews, and the *Star Trek* titles. They also distribute a wide range of group titles from the business books of The Free Press to Nancy Drew and the Hardy Boys titles. Their current list of imprints includes Martin Books,

Archway Paperbacks, Pocket Books, Simon & Schuster, Fireside, and Touchstone. S&S UK imprints also include S&S Audio, the S&S Children's imprints, and Scribner, which is used in the UK for an indigenous literary trade-paperback list. Over the last five years, S&S UK has been one of the fastest growing trade publishers in Britain.

S&S Australia recently acquired Kangaroo Press, a publisher of illustrated craft and gardening books, and the company's other imprint is S&S Australia, which publishes original titles.

HARVEY PENICK'S LITTLE RED BOOK

Lessons and Teachings from a Lifetime in Golf

INTRODUCTIONS BY TOM KITE, BEN CRENSHAW, MICKEY WRIGHT, KATHY WHITWORTH, BETSY RAWLS, MARY LENA FAULK, DAVE MARR, AND BYRON NELSON

HARVEY PENICK *with* BUD SHRAKE

The Christmas Box

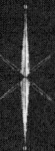

Richard Paul Evans

ACQUISITION FEVER

◩

In the 1980s, as S&S expanded through internal growth, it simultaneously entered a period of aggressive acquisition. In February 1984, it bought Esquire, Inc., a publisher of textbooks and supplementary materials. In December of the same year, S&S bought Prentice-Hall, one of the biggest acquisitions the publishing industry had seen to date. The purchase made S&S a major college-textbook publisher and provided it with an entree into the business and professional publishing markets.

In June 1985, S&S acquired another publisher, Ginn & Company, which published textbooks for elementary school students. Less than one year later, S&S bought Silver Burdett, which led to the formation of Silver Burdett Ginn, a publisher of textbook and related material for grades K–8. In 1990, S&S bought Computer Curriculum Corp. Then, in 1994, S&S made its final major acquisition by purchasing Macmillan's college, trade, reference, and children's units. Simon & Schuster Inc., had become a global multimedia company, the largest English-language publisher in the world.

During this period of intense acquisition, S&S purchased more than 60 companies [see below for a complete list of acquisitions], and revenues rose from $200 million in 1983 to more than $2 billion in 1997.

The purchase of Macmillan brought two additional publishing units under the umbrella of the Simon & Schuster Trade Division—Scribner and The Free Press.

S&S ACQUISITIONS [1984–1997]

Consumer

1984   Stratemeyer Syndicate

1990   Green Tiger Press

1994   Macmillan, Inc., Children's imprints

> Macmillan
> Atheneum Books
> Bradbury Press
> Four Winds Press
> Charles Scribner's Sons
> Margaret K. McElderry Books
> Aladdin
> Collier Books for Young Readers
> Crestwood House
> Dillon Press

Macmilllan, Inc., Adult imprints

> Macmillan
> Charles Scribner's Sons
> Atheneum Books
> Rawson Associates
> Robert Stewart Books
> Howell Book House
> Lisa Drew Books

1996   Kangaroo Press

1997   Pimsleur

Education

1984	Prentice-Hall, Inc.
	Esquire, Inc. (Allyn & Bacon)
1985	Ginn & Company
1986	Silver Burdett
	Lange Medical (renamed Appleton & Lange)
	Yourdon Press
	Grune & Stratton
	Xerox Customized Publishing
1987	CCD Online
	W. C. Brown
1988	Quercus Corporation
	Emanuel Rosenfeld
	T. H. Peek
	Gardener Press
	National Publishers
	International Human Resources Development Inc.
1989	David S. Lake
	Vacation Church School Program
	Janus Book Publishers
	Alemany Press
	Computer Curriculum Corporation (CCC)
1991	Morton Emergency Medical Services
1992	Titles from Elsevier Science Publishing
1994	Macmillan, Inc.
	Macmillan College Publishing
	Merrill Publishing
1995	Educational Management Group (EMG)
	Ziff Davis Press
	Aegian Communications
1996	Cobblestone Publishing Company
	Mergent Technologies (Invest Learning)
	The Waite Group
1997	Gorsuch Scarisbrick
	IRI/Skylight Training and Publishing
	Dothen Healthcare Press
	Young Physician's Journal

Business & Professional

1987	Regents Publishing
1988	Master Data Center
	Clinical Nursing Skills
1989	McGraw-Hill's accounting and auditing titles
	New York Institute of Finance (NYIF)
1994	Macmilllan, Inc.
	Macmillan
	Schirmer
	G. K. Hall
	Jossey-Bass
	Charles Scribner's Sons
	Twayne
	Thorndike Press
	Brassey's
1996	Jossey-Bass acquires Pfeiffer & Co.
1997	Macmillan Reference acquires Menasha Press's *Unofficial Guides*

International

1985	Ginn Canada
1987	Woodhead-Faulkner
1988	Harvester Press Ltd.
	Wheatsheaf Books Ltd.
1989	Ellis Horwood
	Philip Allan
	Macdonald & Co. Children's division
	Macmillan Publishers' ELT list
	Markt & Technik
	Marian DeWett Publishing

Scribner

With the purchase of Macmillan, the adult trade publishing imprints of Macmillan, Charles Scribner's Sons, Atheneum, Lisa Drew Books, and Rawson Associates were brought into the S&S Trade Division. These five imprints were merged into a single hardcover imprint that retains one of the oldest and most resonant names in American publishing, Scribner.

Founded in 1846 by Charles Scribner and Isaac Baker, the Scribner company first published religious books. Baker died in 1850, and Scribner continued alone. In addition to publishing books, Scribner published several magazines, the most famous being *Scribner's Monthly* (1870–1881), "an illustrated magazine for the people." The magazine and its successor, *Scribner's Magazine* (1887–1939), attracted fresh young writers who also wrote books for the company.

Charles Scribner II took over in 1879 after the deaths of his father and older brother, and under his guidance, the company became identified with the giants of twentieth-century American literature, such as Henry James and Edith Wharton. In short succession, Charles Scribner's Sons published Ring Lardner, Ernest Hemingway, Thomas Wolfe, and Marjorie Kinnan Rawlings. Famed editors Maxwell Perkins and John Hall Wheelock realized that a new era in American literature was dawning, and in 1920, F. Scott Fitzgerald's first novel, *This Side of Paradise,* proclaimed the Jazz Age.

In 1978 Scribner acquired Atheneum, publishers of Edward Albee, Charles Johnson, and Theodore H. White. The Atheneum acquisition also brought with it the Rawson Associates imprint. And in 1984, the Scribner Book Companies, which by then included a great children's division and a distinguished reference division, merged with Macmillan.

Today, under publisher Susan Moldow and editor in chief Nan Graham, Scribner has a distinguished list of writers that includes Annie Proulx, whose novel *The Shipping News* (1993) won both the Pulitzer Prize and the National Book Award; Frank McCourt, whose memoir, *Angela's Ashes* (1996), became a mainstay of the *New York Times* bestseller list and was awarded the Pulitzer Prize and the National Book Critics Circle Award; and Don DeLillo, whose novel, *Underworld* (1997), was published to high praise. Scribner has also launched the newly revised *Joy of Cooking,* and, with *Déjà Dead,* introduced a new writer, Kathy Reichs. With the publication of *Bag of Bones* by Stephen King and *Single & Single* by John le Carré, Scribner has brought new readers to well-established and successful writers.

The Free Press

Fp ᖴᑭ ƒP

ounded in 1947 by Jeremiah Kaplan and Charles Leibman, The Free Press of Glencoe, as it was first named, began by specializing in books on the social sciences. Kaplan and his successors published books for educated readers that were intended to take the work of scholars and make them available to a larger public. By the 1950s, there was a growing general readership for such titles as *Love Is Not Enough* by Bruno Bettelheim and *After Divorce* by William J. Goode.

In 1960, The Free Press was bought by the Crowell-Collier Publishing Company and merged with Macmillan, where it became an academic and reference imprint. Throughout the '70s, The Free Press continued to publish books that questioned conventional wisdom, including *The Denial of Death* by Ernest Becker, which won the Pulitzer Prize in 1974. The Free Press began to identify new areas of scholarship and develop a more competitive presence in the retail trade, and, as the boom in MBA education began, it launched a list of titles for professional managers. *Competitive Strategy* (1980), Michael Porter's first in a series of influential business books, leads a list of extremely successful business books.

In the '80s, under publisher Erwin Glikes, The Free Press began an era characterized by controversy. Such titles as *The Tempting of America* by Robert Bork, *Intercourse* by Andrea Dworkin, *The Moral Sense* by James Q. Wilson, *The Tyranny of the Majority* by Lani Guinier, *Denying the Holocaust* by Deborah Lipstadt, *Illiberal Education* by Dinesh D'Souza, and *The Bell Curve* by Richard Herrnstein and Charles Murray touched off intense public debates.

Today, under publisher Paula Barker Duffy and editorial director Elizabeth Maguire, The Free Press continues to publish topical books such as *Spin Cycle* by Howard Kurtz and *The Death of Outrage* by William Bennett. *Ernie Pyle's War* by James Tobin won the National Book Critics Circle Award in 1998, and Free Press business books continue to win awards and lead the field. The Free Press has broadened its editorial scope and now publishes not only influential books in the social sciences, business, and public affairs, but also books from science and newer areas of inquiry such as women's studies.

More Changes

S imon & Schuster was not the only company participating in the feverish climate of media acquisitions. In 1994, shortly after the Macmillan acquisition, Viacom Inc. purchased S&S's parent company, Paramount Communications (the name taken by Gulf +

Western on April 10, 1989). Soon after the Viacom takeover, Snyder left Simon & Schuster, and Jon Newcomb, S&S's president and chief operating officer, assumed the position of chief executive officer. In 1998, a year that would see many publishing mergers and acquisitions, Viacom Inc. sold the educational, professional, business, and reference publishing units of Simon & Schuster Inc. to Pearson Plc., the British publishing conglomerate.

❧ Jon Newcomb.

Jack Romanos.

BEGINNING AGAIN

A s Simon & Schuster, Inc., grew in size and complexity with the many acquisitions through the '80s and early '90s, the trade division experienced further management changes and reorganization. When Charles Hayward was named president of the trade division in 1987, he brought in Jack McKeown as publisher. In 1991, Jack Romanos was named president of the newly formed Consumer Group. And in 1992, Romanos brought in Carolyn Reidy as the president and publisher of the Simon & Schuster Trade Division. During Reidy's tenure the division's revenues have doubled. Today, the trade division includes three hardcover publishing imprints: Simon & Schuster, Scribner, and The Free Press, as well as the four imprints of Simon & Schuster Trade Paperbacks. Kaplan Books, an imprint that publishes test preparation books, is a copublishing program that was begun in 1997 with Kaplan Educational Testing. In 1997, Reidy named David Rosenthal publisher of the Simon & Schuster imprint.

Today, with Jon Newcomb as CEO and Jack Romanos as president and COO, Simon & Schuster Inc. is made up of the international divisions Simon & Schuster UK and Simon & Schuster Australia, and four U.S. divisions: Pocket Books, S&S Children's Publishing, S&S New Media, and S&S Trade.

With the 1998 divestiture of the professional, educational, business, international, and reference units, S&S is once again a dedicated publisher of books for the general reader and comes full circle at the time of its seventy-fifth anniversary. Today, the company is three times larger, and far stronger, than it was before the acquisition period began.

A company started by two young men seventy-five years ago with a puzzle book now publishes more than 2,100 titles annually under thirty-five well-known imprints. Throughout the years, and in every facet of the book-making process, Simon & Schuster has prospered. And it remains the company that Dick Simon and Max Schuster conceived it to be—one committed to publishing quality books in a wide variety of genres and formats for the general reader.

APPENDIXES

Company Organization

POCKET BOOKS
Archway Paperbacks
Folger Shakespeare Library
Minstrel Books
MTV Books
Pocket Books
Pocket Books Hardcover
Pocket Books Trade Paperbacks
Pocket Star Books
Star Trek
Washington Square Press

SIMON & SCHUSTER CHILDREN'S PUBLISHING
Aladdin Paperback
Atheneum Books for Young Readers
    Anne Schwartz Books
    Jean Karl Books
Little Simon
    Simon Spotlight
Margaret K. McElderry Books
Simon & Schuster Books for Young Readers

SIMON & SCHUSTER NEW MEDIA
Simon & Schuster Audio
    Pimsleur
    Simon & Schuster Audioworks
    Simon & Schuster Sound Ideas
    Success
Simon & Schuster Interactive

SIMON & SCHUSTER ONLINE
SimonSays.com

SIMON & SCHUSTER TRADE DIVISION
Simon & Schuster
    Simon & Schuster Editions
Scribner
    Lisa Drew Books
The Free Press
Simon & Schuster Trade Paperbacks
    Fireside
    Touchstone
    Scribner Paperback Fiction
    Libros en Español
Affiliate Publishers
    Kaplan Publishing
    Kaplan Books

SIMON & SCHUSTER UK
Archway Paperbacks
Martin Books
Pocket Books
Simon & Schuster
Scribner
Touchstone
Fireside
Simon & Schuster Audio

SIMON & SCHUSTER AUSTRALIA
Archway Paperbacks
Kangaroo Press
Martin Books
Pocket Books
Simon & Schuster Australia
Touchstone
Fireside

S&S Business Chronology

1924   Richard L. Simon and M. Lincoln Schuster found the company

1930   Leon Shimkin becomes an equal partner

1939   Simon, Schuster, Shimkin, and Robert Fair de Graff start Pocket Books

1944   Simon & Schuster and Pocket Books sold to Marshall Field

1957   Marshall Field dies, and Simon, Schuster, and Shimkin buy back Simon & Schuster. Shimkin and James M. Jacobson buy back Pocket Books. Richard E. Simon retires, Max Schuster and Leon Shimkin buy his shares of Simon & Schuster

1960   Richard L. Simon dies

1961   Pocket Books goes public with Shimkin holding 46 percent of the stock

1966   M. Lincoln Schuster retires. Leon Shimkin acquires Schuster's shares in the company and merges Simon & Schuster and Pocket Books, renaming the company Simon & Schuster, Inc.

1970   M. Lincoln Schuster dies

1975   Leon Shimkin sells Simon & Schuster, Inc., to Gulf + Western and retires

1984   Simon & Schuster begins period of acquisitions (see box on page 72)

1988   Leon Shimkin dies

1989   Gulf + Western restructures and becomes Paramount Communications

1994   Paramount Communications acquired by Viacom

1998   Simon & Schuster's Education, International, Business, Professional and Reference groups sold to Pearson Plc., and Simon & Schuster Inc. is once again solely a publisher of books for the general reader

Awards and Prizes

PULITZER PRIZES

Simon & Schuster
- 1935: Fiction, *Now in November,* Josephine Johnson
- 1967: Biography, *Mr. Clemens and Mark Twain,* Justin Kaplan
- 1968: Nonfiction, *Rousseau and Revolution,* Will and Ariel Durant
- 1986: Fiction, *Lonesome Dove,* Larry McMurtry
- 1988: Nonfiction, *The Making of the Atomic Bomb,* Richard Rhodes
- 1989: History, *Parting the Waters,* Taylor Branch
- 1992: Nonfiction, *The Prize,* Daniel Yergin
- 1993: Nonfiction, *Lincoln at Gettysburg,* Garry Wills
- 1993: Biography, *Truman,* David McCullough
- 1995: History, *No Ordinary Time,* Doris Kearns Goodwin

Scribner
- 1994: Fiction, *The Shipping News,* E. Annie Proulx
- 1997: Biography, *Angela's Ashes,* Frank McCourt

Charles Scribner's Sons, Macmillan, Atheneum
- 1917: History, *With Americans of Past and Present Day,* J.J. Jusserand (Scribner)
- 1918: History, *A History of the Civil War,* James Ford Rhodes (Macmillan)
- 1918: Novel, *His Family,* Ernest Poole (Macmillan)
- 1920: History, *The War with Mexico,* Justin H. Smith (Macmillan)
- 1921: Biography, *The Americanization of Edward Bok,* Edward Bok (Scribner)

1922: Poetry, *Collected Poems,* Edwin Arlington Robinson (Macmillan)

1922: Biography, *A Daughter of the Middle Border,* Hamlin Garland (Macmillan)

1924: Biography, *From Immigrant to Inventor,* Michael Idvorsky Pupin (Scribner)

1924: History, *The American Revolution,* Charles H. McIlwain (Macmillan)

1925: Poetry, *The Man Who Died Twice,* Edwin Arlington Robinson (Macmillan)

1926: History, *A History of the United States,* Edward Channing (Macmillan)

1928: Poetry, *Tristram,* Edwin Arlington Robinson (Macmillan)

1931: History, *The Coming of the War,* Bernadotte E. Schmitt (Scribner)

1935: Biography, *R. E. Lee,* Douglas S. Freeman (Scribner)

1936: Drama, *Idiots Delight,* Robert E. Sherwood (Scribner)

1937: Novel, *Gone with the Wind,* Margaret Mitchell (Macmillan)

1938: Poetry, *Cold Morning Sky,* Marya Zaturenska (Macmillan)

1939: Drama, *Abe Lincoln in Illinois,* Robert E. Sherwood (Scribner)

1939: Novel, *The Yearling,* Marjorie Kinnan Rawlings (Scribner)

1941: Drama, *There Shall Be No Night,* Robert E. Sherwood (Scribner)

1941: Biography, *Jonathan Edwards,* Ola Elizabeth Winslow (Macmillan)

1947: Biography, *The Autobiography of William Allen White,* William Allen White (Macmillan)

1948: Fiction, *Tales of the South Pacific,* James A. Michener (Macmillan)

1949: Poetry, *Terror and Decorum,* Peter Viereck (Scribner)

1952: Poetry, *Collected Poems,* Marianne Moore (Macmillan)

1952: Biography, *Charles Evans Hughes,* Merlo J. Pusey (Macmillan)

1953: Fiction, *The Old Man and the Sea,* Ernest Hemingway (Scribner)

1954: Biography, *The Spirit of St. Louis,* Charles A. Lindbergh (Scribner)

1958: Biography, *George Washington,* Vols. I-VI, Douglas Southall Freeman (Scribner)

1959: History, *The Republican Era: 1869–1901,* Leonard D. White and Jean Schneider (Macmillan)

1962: General Nonfiction, *The Making of the President, 1960,* Theodore H. White (Atheneum)

1967: Drama, *A Delicate Balance,* Edward Albee (Atheneum)

1968: Poetry, *The Hard Hours,* Anthony Hecht (Atheneum)

1969: General Nonfiction, *So Human an Animal,* Rene Jules Dubos (Scribner)

1970: Poetry, *Untitled Subjects,* Richard Howard (Atheneum)

1972: History, *Neither Black nor White,* Carl N. Degler (Macmillan)

1973: Drama, *That Championship Season,* Jason Miller (Atheneum)

1975: Drama, *Seascape,* Edward Albee (Atheneum)

1980: Poetry, *Selected Poems,* Donald Justice (Atheneum)

NATIONAL BOOK AWARDS

Simon & Schuster

1961: Nonfiction, *The Rise and Fall of the Third Reich,* William Shirer

1967: Arts and Letters, *Mr. Clemens and Mark Twain,* Justin Kaplan

1978: History, *The Path Between the Seas,* David McCullough

1981: Biography, *Walt Whitman,* Justin Kaplan

1982: Biography, *Mornings on Horseback,* David McCullough

1987: History, *The Making of the Atomic Bomb,* Richard Rhodes

1994: Fiction, *A Frolic of His Own,* William Gaddis (Poseidon)

Charles Scribner's Sons, Macmillan, Atheneum

1986: Nonfiction, *Arctic Dreams,* Barry Lopez (Scribner)

1990:   Fiction, *Middle Passage,* Charles Johnson (Atheneum)
1994:   Fiction, *The Shipping News,* E. Annie Proulx (Scribner)

NATIONAL BOOK CRITICS CIRCLE AWARDS

Simon & Schuster

1983:   Nonfiction, *The Price of Power,* Seymour M. Hersh
        (Summit)
1987:   Nonfiction, *The Making of the Atomic Bomb,* Richard
        Rhodes
1988:   Nonfiction, *Parting the Waters,* Taylor Branch
1992:   Criticism, *Lincoln at Gettysburg,* Garry Wills
1998:   Biography, *A Beautiful Mind,* Sylvia Nasar

Scribner

1996: Autobiography, *Angela's Ashes,* Frank McCourt

Bestseller Lists

TRADE DIVISION BESTSELLERS*

～ SIMON & SCHUSTER

1924

The Cross Word Puzzle Books by F. Gregory Hartswick, Prosper Buranelli, and Margaret Petherbridge

1926

The Story of Philosophy by Will Durant
Transition by Will Durant

1927

Trader Horn, Vol. I, by Alfred Aloysius Horn and Ethelreda Lewis

1929

The Art of Thinking by Ernest Dimnet
The Cradle of the Deep by Joan Lowell
Believe It or Not by Robert L. Ripley
The Mansions of Philosophy by Will Durant

*List compiled from *Publishers Weekly* hardcover bestseller list, since its inception in 1919; and the *New York Times* hardcover list since its beginnings in 1935. Titles that appeared in more than one year are listed only in the year in which they first appeared on the list.

1930

The Cross Word Puzzle Book: Series 16 by F. Gregory Hartswick,
Prosper Buranelli, and Margaret Petherbridge
Caught Short by Eddie Cantor
Men of Art by Thomas Craven

1931

Hard Lines by Ogden Nash

1932

Van Loon's Geography by Hendrik Willem Van Loon
What We Live By by Ernest Dimnet
A New Way to Better Golf by Alex J. Morrison

1933

Little Man, What Now? by Hans Fallada
More Power to You by Walter B. Pitkin
Money Contract by P. Hal Sims
The First World War, Laurence Stallings, ed.

the Story of Civilization

THE LIFE
OF
GREECE

WILL DURANT

A history of Greek government, industry, manners, morals, religion, philosophy, science, literature, and art from the earliest times to the Roman conquest

1934

Nijinsky by Romola Nijinsky
The Coming American Boom by Lawrence Angas
Modern Art by Thomas Craven
The Life of Our Lord by Charles Dickens
More Careers for Youth by Walter B. Pitkin
The New Dealers by Unofficial Observer

1935

The Story of Civilization by Will Durant
Now in November by Josephine Winslow Johnson
Inflation Ahead! by W. M. Kiplinger and Frederick Shelton
The Art of Happiness by John C. Powys
Farewell to Fifth Avenue by Cornelius Vanderbilt, Jr.
Ships by Hendrik Willem Van Loon
Around the World with the Alphabet by Hendrik Willem Van Loon

1936

Wake Up and Live! by Dorothea Brande
I Write as I Please by Walter Duranty

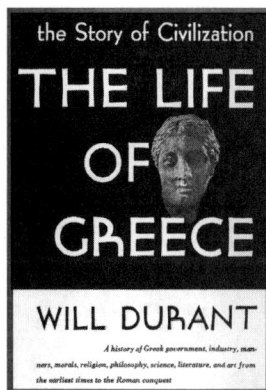

Simon & Schuster bestsellers, continued

The Cross Word Puzzle Book: Series 39 by F. Gregory Hartswick,
Prosper Buranelli, and Margaret Petherbridge
What's This? by Milt Gross
Green Laurels by Donald Culross Peattie
Your Income Tax by Hugh Satterlee and I. H. Sher
The Coming Boom in Real Estate by Roy Wenzlick

1937

How to Win Friends & Influence People by Dale Carnegie
The Arts by Hendrik Willem Van Loon
The Bible, Designed to Be Read as Living Literature, Ernest
Sutherland Bates, ed.
Away from It All by Cedric Belfrage
The Outward Room by Millen Brand

1938

With Malice Toward Some by Margaret Halsey
The World Is Mine by William James Blech
Designing Women by Margaretta Byers and Consuelo
Kamholz
Danger Is My Business by John D. Craig
Five Suit Bridge, Ely Culbertson, ed.
The Evolution of Physics by Albert Einstein and Leopold Infeld
Of Men and Music by Deems Taylor
Christmas Carols by Hendrik Willem Van Loon and Grace
Castagnetta

1939

We Saw It Happen by Hanson Weightman Baldwin, et al.
The Heroes by Millen Brand
A Treasury of Art Masterpieces, Thomas Craven, ed.
Grandma Called It Carnal by Bertha Damon
I Believe, Clifton Fadiman, ed.
How to Raise a Dog by James R. Kinney and Ann Honeycutt
Daily Except Sunday by Edward Streeter

Address Unknown by Kressman Taylor
Our Battle by Hendrik Willem Van Loon

1940

How to Read a Book by Mortimer Adler
American White Paper by Joseph W.
  Alsop, Jr., and Robert Kinter
King's Row by Henry Bellamann
M-Day by Leo M. Cherne
Mathematics and the Imagination by Edward
  Kasner and James Newman
The Well-Tempered Listener by Deems Taylor

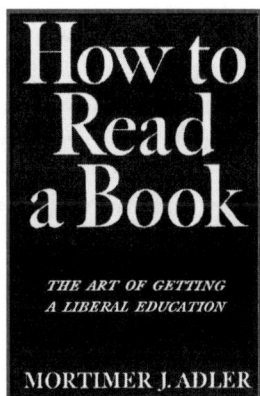

How to Read a Book

THE ART OF GETTING
A LIBERAL EDUCATION

MORTIMER J. ADLER

1941

Reading I've Liked, Clifton Fadiman, ed.
J. K. Lasser's Your Income Tax by J.K. Lasser Tax Institute
A Treasury of the World's Great Letters, M. Lincoln Schuster, ed.
A Treasury of Gilbert and Sullivan by Deems Taylor

1942

The Floods of Spring by Henry Bellamann
Mission to Moscow by Joseph E. Davies
Victory Through Air Power by Major Alexander P. De Seversky
City Lawyer by Arthur Garfield Hays
How War Came by Ernest Lindley and Forrest Davis
War and Peace by Lyev N. Tolstoy
Reprisal by Ethel Vance
Van Loon's Lives by Hendrik Willem Van Loon

1943

One World by Wendell L. Willkie
A Sense of Humus by Bertha Damon
Release from Nervous Tension by David Harold Fink, M.D.
Report from Tokyo by Joseph C. Grew
The Trespassers by Laura Z. Hobson
I Am Thinking of My Darling by Vincent McHugh
Roughly Speaking by Louise Randall Pierson
Equinox by Alan Seager

Simon & Schuster bestsellers, continued

1944

I Never Left Home by Bob Hope
Ten Years in Japan by Joseph C. Grew
How to Think About War and Peace by Mortimer J. Adler
Target: Germany—The Army Air Force's Official Story
Man in the Shower by Peter Arno
Victoria Grandolet by Henry Bellamann
Avalanche by Kay Boyle
Some of My Best Friends Are Soldiers by Margaret Halsey
The Ten Commandments, Armin L. Robinson, ed.
A Pictorial History of the Movies by Deems Taylor, Marcelene
    Peterson, and Bryant Hale

1945

Try and Stop Me by Bennett Cerf
General Marshall's Report by Gen. George C. Marshall
The Sad Sack by Sgt. George Baker
Enrico Caruso by Dorothy Caruso
On a Note of Triumph by Norman Corwin
Caesar and Christ by Will Durant
The Happy Time by Robert Louis Fontaine
Carrier War by Lt. Oliver Jenson
Dark Medallion by Dorothy Langley
Tomorrow's House by George Nelson and Henry M. Wright
Sixty Million Jobs by Henry A. Wallace
American Guerrilla in the Philippines by Ira Wolfert

1946

Peace of Mind by Joshua L. Liebman
My Three Years with Eisenhower by Capt. Harry C. Butcher
So This Is Peace by Bob Hope
We Happy Few by Helen Huntington Howe
Night and the City by Gerald Kersh
A History of Western Philosophy by Bertrand Russell
Days and Nights by Konstantin Mikhailovich Simonov

Starling of the White House by Col. Edmund Starling and Thomas Sugrue

1947

Gentleman's Agreement by Laura Z. Hobson
Peace of Mind by Joshua L. Liebman
The Fireside Book of Folk Songs, Margaret B. Boni, ed.
The American Past by Roger Butterfield
How Green Was My Father by David Dodge
Mr. Blandings Builds His Dream House by Eric Hodgins
Reilly of the White House by Michael Francis Reilly, as told to William J. Slocum
The Golden History of the World by Jane Werner Watson
Aurora Dawn by Herman Wouk

1948

How to Stop Worrying and Start Living by Dale Carnegie
Parris Mitchell of King's Row by Henry Bellamann and Katherine Bellamann
The Mind in Action by Eric Berne
Westward Ha! by S. J. Perelman
Never Love a Stranger by Harold Robbins
Wine, Women, and Words by Billy Rose

1949

Father of the Bride by Edward Streeter
The Life and Times of the Shmoo by Al Capp
Shake Well Before Using by Bennett Cerf
Frenchman: A Photographic Interview by Philippe Halsman
The Aspirin Age 1919–1941, Isabel Leighton, ed.
An Act of Love by Ira Wolfert

1950

The Cardinal by Henry Morton Robinson
Presidents Who Have Known Me by George Edward Allen
Life's Picture History of World War II

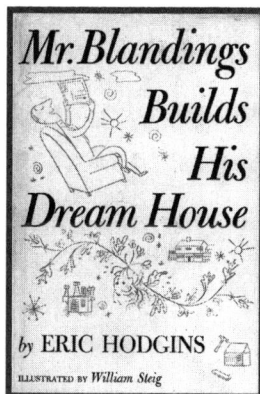

Simon & Schuster bestsellers, continued

Modern Arms and Free Men by Vannevar Bush
Homeward Borne by Ruth Chatterton
The Other Father by Laura Z. Hobson
The Circle of the Day by Helen Huntington Howe

1951

Pogo by Walt Kelly
The Story of The New York Times by Meyer Berger
Mary Garden's Story by Mary Garden and Louis Biancolli
The Celebrity by Laura Z. Hobson
The Pedlocks by Stephen Longstreet
My Mission in Israel by James Grover McDonald
Unpopular Essays by Bertrand Russell
The 13 Clocks by James Thurber

1952

The Baby
Walt Disney's Story Book of Peter Pan
The Herblock Book by Herbert Block
The Fireside Book of Favorite American Songs, Margaret B.
   Boni, ed.
I Go Pogo by Walt Kelly
How to Succeed in Business Without Really Trying by E. S. Mead
The Thurber Album by James Thurber
Stories from Mary Poppins by Pamela L. Travers
The Golden Geography by Jane Werner Watson

1953

This I Believe, Edward R. Murrow, ed.
How to Play Your Best Golf All the Time by Tommy Armour
Call Me Lucky by Bing Crosby and Pete Martin
The Renaissance by Will Durant
The Secret Diary of Harold L. Ickes by Harold L. Ickes
Zorba the Greek by Nikos Kazantzakis
Uncle Pogo So-So Stories by Walt Kelly

Satan in the Suburbs by Bertrand Russell
Anyone's My Name by Seymour Shubin
Thurber Country by James Thurber

1954

The Saturday Evening Post *Treasury,* Roger Butterfield, ed.
A Philosophy for Our Time by Bernard M. Baruch
The Wilder Shores of Love by Lesley Blanch
Walt Disney's Treasury by Steffu Fletcher and Jane Werner Watson
Journey to the Far Amazon by Alain Gheerbrant
The Journal of Edwin Carp by Richard Haydn
A Child of the Century by Ben Hecht
The Secret Diary of Harold L. Ickes, Vol. II, by Harold Ickes
The Greek Passion by Nikos Kazantzakis
The Incompleat Pogo by Walt Kelly
This I Believe 2, Edward R. Murrow and Raymond Swing, eds.
The Art of Advocacy by Lloyd Paul Stryker
The Golden Bible for Children by Jane Werner Watson

1955

The Man in the Gray Flannel Suit by Sloan Wilson
Walt Disney's Lady and the Tramp
Walt Disney's Davy Crockett by Elizabeth Beecher
Walt Disney's 20,000 Leagues Under the Sea by Elizabeth Beecher
Have Tux, Will Travel by Bob Hope
The Family of Man by Edward Steichen
The Last Temptation by Joseph Viertel
Walt Disney's Living Desert by Jane Werner Watson
The Game of Hearts by Harriet Wilson

1956

Eloise by Kay Thompson
Love or Perish by Smiley Blanton
Herblock's Here and Now by Herbert Block
The World We Live In by the Editors of *Life*
King of Paris by Guy Endore
The Success by Helen Huntington Howe

The Boy Scientist by John Bryan Lewellen
The Golden Book of Science by Bertha Morris Parker
Thurber's Dogs by James Thurber

1957

Compulsion by Meyer Levin
Eloise in Paris by Kay Thompson
A Legacy by Sybille Bedford
The Reformation by Will Durant
The American Heritage Book of Great Historic Places, Richard M. Ketchum, ed.
Gypsy by Gypsy Rose Lee
No Down Payment by John McPartland
Investors' Road Map by Alice B. Morgan
The Road to Miltown by S. J. Perelman
The Wonderful O by James Thurber
The Organization Man by William H. Whyte

1958

Eloise at Christmastime by Kay Thompson
Purely Academic by Stringfellow Barr
Herblock's Special for Today by Herbert Block
Boys' Life *Treasury* by the Editors of *Boys' Life*
The Roots of Heaven by Gary Romain
Strangers When We Meet by Evan Hunter
The Best of Everything by Rona Jaffe
America as a Civilization by Max Lerner
U.S.A.—Second Class Power? by Drew Pearson and Jack Anderson
Walt Disney's Worlds of Nature by Rutherford Hayes Platt
A Summer Place by Sloan Wilson

The Best of Everything
A NOVEL BY RONA JAFFE

1959

Mine Enemy Grows Older by Alexander King
Spinster by Sylvia Ashton-Warner
California Street by Niven Busch

Yesterday by Maria Dermout
Lady L. by Romain Gary
Eva by Meyer Levin
How I Turned $1,000 into a Million in Real Estate by William Nickerson
The Devil in Bucks County by Edmund Schiddel

1960

The Chapman Report by Irving Wallace
May This House Be Safe from Tigers by Alexander King
The Rise and Fall of the Third Reich by William L. Shirer
The Joy of Music by Leonard Bernstein
Dempsey by Jack Dempsey with Bob Considine and Bill Slocum
Away from Home by Rona Jaffe
Water of Life by Henry Morton Robinson
The Longest Day by Cornelius Ryan
The Last Temptation of Christ by Nikos Kazantzakis

1961

The Carpetbaggers by Harold Robbins
America—Too Young to Die! by Major Alexander P. De Seversky
The Age of Reason Begins by Will and Ariel Durant
Fate Is the Hunter by Ernest K. Gann
The Fifty-Year Decline and Fall of Hollywood by Ezra Goodman
Mothers and Daughters by Evan Hunter
Rizpah by Charles E. Israel
I Should Have Kissed Her More by Alexander King
The Queen's Necklace by Frances Mossiker
Lizzie Borden by Edward D. Radin
Lilith by J. R. Salamanca
The Twenty-seventh Wife by Irving Wallace

1962

The Prize by Irving Wallace
Calories Don't Count by Dr. Herman Taller
The San Franciscans by Niven Busch
The Passion Flower Hotel by Rosalind Erskine
The Decline of Pleasure by Walter Kerr

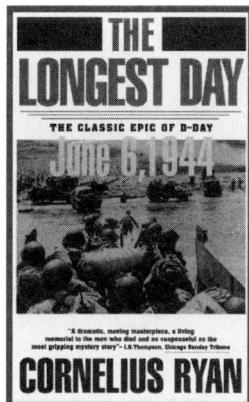

My Sabre Is Bent by Jack Paar
Where Love Has Gone by Harold Robbins
Before My Time by Niccolo Tucci
Capitol Hill by Andrew Tully

1963

Portrait of Myself by Margaret Bourke-White
The Moonflower Vine by Jetta Carleton
The Deed by Gerold Frank
Of Good and Evil by Ernest K. Gann
Is There Life After Birth? by Alexander King
The American Way of Death by Jessica Mitford
The Three Sirens by Irving Wallace

JESSICA MITFORD
The American Way of Death

1964

The Man by Irving Wallace
John Lennon in His Own Write by John Lennon
My Autobiography by Charles Chaplin
A Mother's Kisses by Bruce Jay Friedman
The Fanatic by Meyer Levin
The Green Felt Jungle by Ed Reid and Ovid Demaris (Trident)
Four Days by UPI and American Heritage

1965

Is Paris Burning? by Larry Collins and Dominique Lapierre
A Spaniard in the Works by John Lennon

1966

The Adventurers by Harold Robbins (Trident)
The Secret of Santa Vittoria by Robert Crichton
Everything but Money by Sam Levenson
The Last Battle by Cornelius Ryan
The Kremlin Letter by Noel Behn

1967

The Chosen by Chaim Potok
The Plot by Irving Wallace

A Modern Priest Looks at His Outdated Church by Father James
Kavanaugh (Trident)
The Groucho Letters by Groucho Marx
Treblinka by Jean-Francois Steiner

1968

The Way Things Work
. . . *Or I'll Dress You in Mourning* by Larry Collins and
Dominique Lapierre
Quotations from Chairman LBJ by Lyndon Baines Johnson
The Case Against Congress by Drew Pearson and Jack Anderson
True Grit by Charles Portis

1969

The Love Machine by Jacqueline Susann
The Inheritors by Harold Robbins (Trident)
The Seven Minutes by Irving Wallace
The Inland Island by Josephine Winslow Johnson
The Day of the Dolphin by Robert Merle
The Collapse of the Third Republic by William
L. Shirer
My Turn at Bat by Ted Williams
The Vatican Empire by Nino Lo Bello (Trident)
The Selling of the President by Joe McGinniss
(Trident)

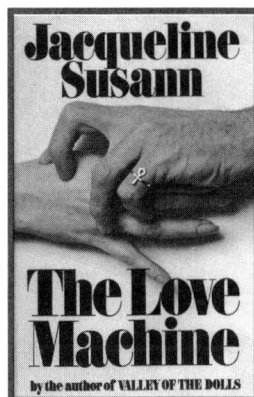

1970

The Game of Nations by Miles Copeland
God Is an Englishman by R. F. Delderfield
From Those Wonderful Folks Who Gave You Pearl Harbor by
Jerry Della Femina and Charles Sopkin
Catch-22 by Joseph Heller
Do It! Scenarios of the Revolution by Jerry Rubin
Sylvester and the Magic Pebble by William Steig

1971

The Betsy by Harold Robbins (Trident)
Crime in America by Ramsey Clark

Simon & Schuster bestsellers, continued

Theirs Was the Kingdom by R. F. Delderfield
The Antagonists by Ernest K. Gann
Penmarric by Susan Howatch

1972

The Word by Irving Wallace
Journey to Ixtlan: The Lessons of Don Juan by Carlos Castaneda
O Jerusalem! by Larry Collins and Dominique Lapierre
To Serve Them All My Days by R. F. Delderfield
The Settlers by Meyer Levin
A Portion for Foxes by Jane McIlvaine McClary
The Betsy by Harold Robbins (Trident)

1973

Once Is Not Enough by Jacqueline Susann
The Honorary Consul by Graham Greene
In One Era and Out the Other by Sam Levenson
Law and Order by Dorothy Uhnak

1974

The Pirate by Harold Robbins
The Fan Club by Irving Wallace
All the President's Men by Carl Bernstein and Bob Woodward
Tales of Power by Carlos Castaneda
Give Us This Day by R. F. Delderfield
Band of Brothers by Ernest K. Gann
Cashelmara by Susan Howatch
The Woman He Loved by Ralph Martin
A Bridge Too Far by Cornelius Ryan

1975

Looking for Mister Goodbar by Judith Rossner
Total Fitness in 30 Minutes a Week by Laurence E. Morehouse and Leonard Gross

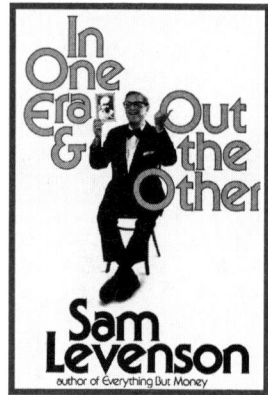

Shardik by Richard Adams
Against Our Will by Susan Brownmiller
Freedom at Midnight by Larry Collins and
    Dominique Lapierre
Nice Guys Finish Last by Leo Durocher and
    Ed Linn
Pumping Iron by Charles Gaines and
    George Butler

1976
The Lonely Lady by Harold Robbins
The Final Days by Carl Bernstein and Bob
    Woodward
Blind Ambition: The White House Years by John Dean
The Age of Napoleon by Will and Ariel Durant
Lovers and Tyrants by Francine du Plessix Gray
The Auctioneer by Joan Samson
A Year of Beauty and Health by Vidal Sassoon and
    Beverly Sassoon with Camille Duhe
The R Document by Irving Wallace

1977
Dreams Die First by Harold Robbins
The Second Ring of Power by Carlos Castaneda
Five Seasons by Roger Angell
Royal Canadian Air Force Exercise Plans for Physical Fitness
A Book of Common Prayer by Joan Didion
Vivien Leigh: A Biography by Anne Edwards
The Crash of '79 by Paul E. Erdman
The Rich Are Different by Susan Howatch
In the National Interest by Marvin Kalb and Ted Koppel
The Gamesman by Michael Maccoby
The Path Between the Seas by David McCullough
Attachments by Judith Rossner
The Investigation by Dorothy Uhnak

1978
The Teamsters by Steven Brill
A Stranger Is Watching by Mary Higgins Clark

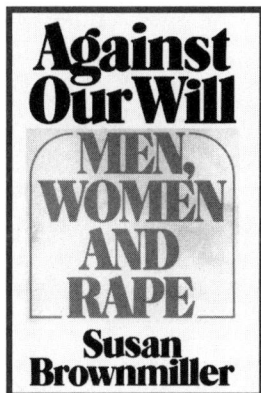

KG 200 by J. D. Gilman and John Clive
The Human Factor by Graham Greene
Tutankhamun by Thomas Hoving
Families by Jane Howard
Arnold: The Education of a Bodybuilder by Arnold Schwarzenegger
  and Douglas Kent Hall
Running and Being by Dr. George A. Sheehan

1979

Memories of Another Day by Harold Robbins
The Brethren: Inside the Supreme Court by Bob
  Woodward and Scott Armstrong
How to Get Everything You Want Out of Life by
  Dr. Joyce Brothers
The White Album by Joan Didion
Good as Gold by Joseph Heller
*You Don't Have to Be in Who's Who to Know
  What's What* by Sam Levenson
*Sideshow: Kissinger, Nixon and the Destruction
  of Cambodia* by William Shawcross
Love & Guilt & the Meaning of Life by Judith Viorst
The Pigeon Project by Irving Wallace

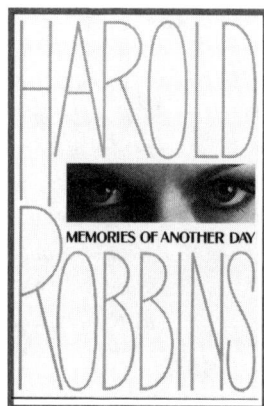

1980

Nothing Down by Robert Allen
The Fifth Horseman by Larry Collins and Dominique Lapierre
Kane & Abel by Jeffrey Archer
The Cradle Will Fall by Mary Higgins Clark
Donahue: My Own Story by Phil Donahue
The Sky's the Limit by Dr. Wayne W. Dyer
A Man by Oriana Fallaci
Doctor Fischer of Geneva or the Bomb Party by Graham Greene
Merv: An Autobiography by Merv Griffin and Peter Barsocchini
Sins of the Fathers by Susan Howatch
Heartsounds by Martha Weinman Lear

A View from a Broad by Bette Midler
Arnold's Bodyshaping for Women by Arnold Schwarzenegger
    and Douglas Kent Hall

1981

Goodbye, Janette by Harold Robbins
Earthly Powers by Anthony Burgess
The Eagle's Gift by Carlos Castaneda
The Last Days of America by Paul E. Erdman
Walt Whitman by Justin Kaplan
Elizabeth Taylor: The Last Star by Kitty Kelley
Mornings on Horseback by David McCullough
The Art of Japanese Management by Richard Tanner Pascale
    and Anthony G. Athos
Maria Callas by Arianna Stassinopoulos
False Witness by Dorothy Uhnak

1982

Jane Fonda's Workout Book by Jane Fonda
Jane Fonda's Workout Book for Pregnancy, Birth, and Recovery
    by Femmy DeLyser
Late Innings by Roger Angell
The Grande Dames by Stephen Birmingham
What Every Woman Should Know About Men by Dr. Joyce Brothers
Strategic Investing by Douglas R. Casey
Lace by Shirley Conran
Witness to Power by John Ehrlichman
Monsignor Quixote by Graham Greene
Spellbinder by Harold Robbins

1983

Hollywood Wives by Jackie Collins
Creating Wealth by Robert G. Allen
The Body Principal by Victoria Principal
The Warlord by Malcolm Bosse
Christie Brinkley's Outdoor Beauty & Fitness Book by Christie Brinkley
Salvador by Joan Didion
Mandarin by Robert S. Elegant

107

APPENDIX

Simon & Schuster bestsellers, continued

Working Out by Charles Hix
Monimbo by Robert Moss and Arnaud de Borchgrave
Confessions of an Actor by Laurence Olivier
The Partners by James B. Stewart

1984

Webster's New World Dictionary, Second College Edition
Knock Wood by Candice Bergen
The Fire from Within by Carlos Castaneda
Stillwatch by Mary Higgins Clark
Past Imperfect by Joan Collins
Deep Six by Clive Cussler
Democracy by Joan Didion
The Wheel of Fortune by Susan Howatch
Life Its Ownself by Dan Jenkins
Mayor: An Autobiography by Edward Koch with William Rauch
Coroner by Dr. Thomas T. Noguchi and Joseph DiMona
The Pritikin Promise by Nathan Pritikin
Descent from Xanadu by Harold Robbins
What's Ahead for the Economy by Louis Rukeyser
Wired: The Short Life and Fast Times of John Belushi by Bob Woodward

1985

Lucky by Jackie Collins
Living with the Kennedys by Marcia Chellis
Fall from Grace by Larry Collins
The Human Animal by Phil Donahue
Less Than Zero by Bret Easton Ellis
Women Coming of Age by Jane Fonda and Mignon McCarthy
Lonesome Dove by Larry McMurtry
Contact by Carl Sagan

1986

Hollywood Husbands by Jackie Collins
Cyclops by Clive Cussler
Pat Nixon: The Untold Story by Julie Nixon Eisenhower

Jane Fonda's New Workout & Weight-Loss Program by Jane Fonda
Wiseguy by Nicholas Pileggi
Regrets Only by Sally Quinn
Unlimited Power by Anthony Robbins
The Storyteller by Harold Robbins
Necessary Losses by Judith Viorst

1987

Veil: The Secret Wars of the CIA, 1981–1987 by Bob Woodward
The Great Depression of 1990 by Ravi Batra
The Closing of the American Mind by Allan Bloom
Dirk Gently's Holistic Detective Agency by Douglas Adams
Weep No More, My Lady by Mary Higgins Clark
The Red White and Blue by John Gregory Dunne
Postcards from the Edge by Carrie Fisher
The Fitzgeralds and the Kennedys by Doris Kearns Goodwin
Night of the Fox by Jack Higgins
Texasville by Larry McMurtry
The Diet Principal by Victoria Principal
A Woman of Egypt by Jehan Sadat

1988

Surviving the Great Depression by Ravi Batra
Almost Golden by Gwenda Blair
Capote by Gerald Clarke
Rock Star by Jackie Collins
Primetime by Joan Collins
Sword Point by Harold Coyle
Treasure by Clive Cussler
The Ragman's Son by Kirk Douglas
They Went That-a-Way by Malcolm Forbes and Jeff Block
Secrets of the Temple by William Greider
Picasso: Creator and Destroyer by Arianna Huffington
Anything for Billy by Larry McMurtry
Willie by Willie Nelson and Bud Shrake
1999: The Global Challenges We Face in the Next Decade by Richard
    M. Nixon

Simon & Schuster bestsellers, continued

1989

While My Pretty One Sleeps by Mary Higgins Clark
Wealth Without Risk: How to Develop a Personal Fortune Without Going Out on a Limb by Charles J. Givens
It's Always Something by Gilda Radner
The Long Dark Tea-Time of the Soul by Douglas Adams
A Twist in the Tale by Jeffrey Archer
Parting the Waters by Taylor Branch
Maze by Larry Collins
About Face: Odyssey of an American Warrior by David Hackworth and Julie Sherman
A Season in Hell by Jack Higgins
Rolling Stone: *The Photographs,* Laurie Kratochvil, ed.
Life Smiles Back by Philip B. Kunhardt, Jr.
One Up on Wall Street by Peter Lynch and John Rothchild
Father and Son by Peter Maas
Some Can Whistle by Larry McMurtry
Symptoms by Isadore Rosenfeld, M.D.
Forever Fifty: And Other Negotiations by Judith Viorst
Shelley II by Shelley Winters

1990

An American Life: An Autobiography by Ronald Reagan
Lady Boss by Jackie Collins
Financial Self-Defense: How to Win the Fight for Financial Freedom by Charles J. Givens
The 7 Habits of Highly Effective People by Stephen R. Covey
Bright Star by Harold Coyle
Dragon by Clive Cussler
How to Make Nothing but Money by Dave Del Dotto
Now You Know by Kitty Dukakis and Jane Scovell
Surrender the Pink by Carrie Fisher
Cold Harbour by Jack Higgins
Slim by Slim Keith with Annette Tapert

Buffalo Girls by Larry McMurtry
Chicka Chicka Boom Boom by Bill Martin, Jr., and John Archambault
In the Arena: A Memoir of Victory, Defeat, and Renewal by Richard M.
    Nixon
The New Pritikin Program by Robert Pritikin
Deceptions by Philip Roth
In All His Glory by Sally Bedell Smith

1991

Loves Music, Loves to Dance by Mary
    Higgins Clark
Nancy Reagan: The Unauthorized Biography
    by Kitty Kelley
More Wealth Without Risk by Charles J. Givens
Den of Thieves by James B. Stewart
The Prize by Daniel Yergin
Patrimony by Philip Roth
The Commanders by Bob Woodward
Muhammad Ali by Thomas Hauser
Ronald Reagan by Ronald Reagan
Boss of Bosses by Joseph O'Brien and Andris Kurins
Under the Influence by Peter Hernon and Terry Ganey
Making the Most of Your Money by Jane Bryant Quinn
Cruel Doubts by Joe McGinniss
Madonna Unauthorized by Christopher Anderson
The Best Treatment by Isadore Rosenfeld, M.D.
The Jordan Blues by Sam Smith
The Eagle Has Flown by Jack Higgins
Piranhas by Harold Robbins

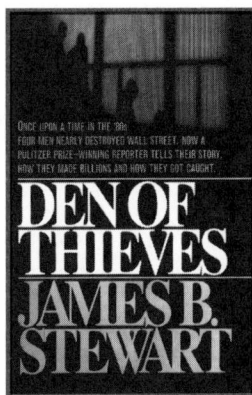

1992

All Around the Town by Mary Higgins Clark
Diana: Her True Story by Andrew Morton
Truman by David McCullough
Seize the Moment by Richard M. Nixon
Who Will Tell the People? by William Greider

Simon & Schuster bestsellers, continued

Lincoln at Gettysburg by Garry Wills
Harvey Penick's Little Red Book by Harvey Penick
Kissinger: A Biography by Walter Isaacson
Trial by Fire by Harold Coyle
Sahara by Clive Cussler
Evening Star by Larry McMurtry
Vanish with the Rose by Barbara Michaels

1993

Private Parts by Howard Stern
Stop the Insanity by Susan Powter
And if You Play Golf, You're My Friend by Harvey Penick with
  Bud Shrake
Making the Mummies Dance by Thomas Hoving
Beating the Street by Peter Lynch
American Star by Jackie Collins
I'll Be Seeing You by Mary Higgins Clark
Streets of Laredo by Larry McMurtry
The Last Brother by Joe McGinniss
Under the Tarnished Dome by Don Yaeger and Douglas S. Looney
The Fountain of Age by Betty Friedan
The Road Less Traveled by M. Scott Peck
Pot of Gold by Judith Michael
The Book of Virtues by William J. Bennett

1994

The Book of Virtues by William J. Bennett
The Lottery Winner by Mary Higgins Clark
Remember Me by Mary Higgins Clark
Inca Gold by Clive Cussler
The Agenda by Bob Woodward
First Things First by Stephen R. Covey and A. Roger Miller
All's Fair: Love, War & Running for President by James Carville
  and Mary Matalin (with Random House)
God's Other Son by Don Imus

D-Day, June 6, 1944 by Stephen E. Ambrose
Diplomacy by Henry Kissinger
No Ordinary Time by Doris Kearns Goodwin
The Tribe of Tiger by Elizabeth Marshall
    Thomas
Hollywood Kids by Jackie Collins

1995

The Christmas Box by Richard Paul Evans
Silent Night by Mary Higgins Clark
The Moral Compass by William J. Bennett
A Good Life by Ben Bradlee
The Children's Book of Virtues by William J.
    Bennett
Food by Susan Powter
From Time to Time by Jack Finney
Let Me Call You Sweetheart by Mary Higgins Clark
Dark Sun by Richard Rhodes
Dead Man's Walk by Larry McMurtry
The Melatonin Miracle by Walter Pierpaoli and William
    Regelson
Lincoln by David Herbert Donald
Shock Wave by Clive Cussler

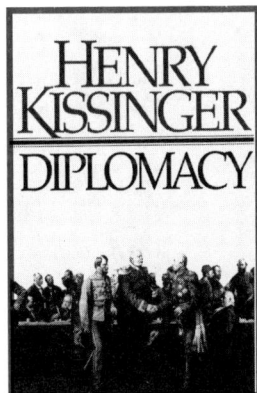

1996

Moonlight Becomes You by Mary Higgins Clark
My Gal Sunday by Mary Higgins Clark
My Story by The Duchess of York
It Takes a Village by Hillary Rodham Clinton
Blood Sport by James B. Stewart
Timepiece by Richard Paul Evans
The Choice by Bob Woodward
Great Books by David Denby
Hit & Run by Nancy Griffin and Kim Masters
Reasonable Doubts by Alan M. Dershowitz
The Sea Hunters by Clive Cussler and Craig Dirgo
Undaunted Courage by Stephen E. Ambrose

Simon & Schuster bestsellers, continued

1997

Pretend You Don't See Her by Mary Higgins Clark
Diana: Her True Story by Andrew Morton
The Letter by Richard Paul Evans
Flood Tide by Clive Cussler
The Bible Code by Michael Drosnin
Three Wishes by Barbara Delinsky
The Road Less Traveled and Beyond by M. Scott Peck
Comanche Moon by Larry McMurtry
Wait Till Next Year by Doris Kearns Goodwin
Citizen Soldiers by Stephen E. Ambrose

1998

The Victors by Stephen Ambrose
Pillar of Fire by Taylor Branch
. . . And the Horse He Rode in On by James Carville
All Through the Night by Mary Higgins Clark
You Belong to Me by Mary Higgins Clark
Thrill! by Jackie Collins
Coast Road by Barbara Delinsky
The Roaring 2000s by Harry S. Dent
The Locket by Richard Paul Evans
Diana: Portrait of a Princess by Jayne Fincher
Bitter Harvest by Ann Rule
In the Meantime by Iyanla Vanzant

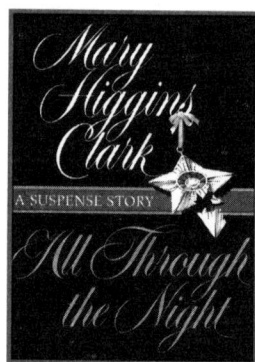

❧ FIRESIDE

1974

The Joy of Sex by Alex Comfort

1976

More Joy of Sex by Alex Comfort

1981

Shout! by Philip Norman

114

1982

Chuck & Di Have a Baby by John Boswell with Patty Brown and Will Elder

1987

A Season on the Brink by John Feinstein

1989

Life Smiles Back by Philip B. Kunhardt, Jr.

1990

The 7 Habits of Highly Effective People by Stephen R. Covey
The Clothes Have No Emperor by Paul Slansky

1993

Teaching Your Children Values by Linda Eyre

1994

Money Doesn't Grow on Trees by Neale S. Godfrey
The Pocket Powter by Susan Powter

1996

First Things First by Stephen R. Covey

1998

One Day My Soul Just Opened Up by Iyanla Vanzant
The Seat of the Soul by Gary Zukav

❧ TOUCHSTONE

1975

Tales of Power by Carlos Castaneda

1976

Curtain by Agatha Christie

1980

Babysitter by Andrew Coburn

1982

The Eagle's Gift by Carlos Castaneda

Touchstone bestsellers, continued

1984

People of the Lie by M. Scott Peck

1985

The New Our Bodies, Our Selves by The Boston Women's Health Book Collective

The Fire from Within by Carlos Castaneda

The Road Less Traveled by M. Scott Peck

1988

The Closing of the American Mind by Allan Bloom

1990

The Pandora Principle by Carolyn Clowes

1993

Truman by David McCullough

Den of Thieves by James B. Stewart

Lincoln at Gettysburg by Garry Wills

The Prize by Daniel Yergin

1994

Schindler's List by Thomas Keneally

Further Along the Road Less Traveled by M. Scott Peck

The Shipping News by E. Annie Proulx

The Longest Day by Cornelius Ryan

1995

No Ordinary Time by Doris Kearns Goodwin

The Shipping News by E. Annie Proulx

1996

We're Right, They're Wrong by James Carville and Mary Matalin (with Random House)

It Takes a Village by Hillary Rodham Clinton

1997

Undaunted Courage by Stephen E. Ambrose

1998

    Citizen Soldiers by Stephen E. Ambrose
    D-Day, June 6, 1944 by Stephen E. Ambrose
    The Bible Code by Michael Drosnin
    Wait Till Next Year by Doris Kearns Goodwin

SCRIBNER PAPERBACK FICTION

1996

    Stones from the River by Ursula Hegi

SCRIBNER

1994

    The Body Farm by Patricia Boswell
    Barbara Bush: A Memoir by Barbara Bush

1995

    From Potter's Field by Patricia Cornwell
    Mindhunter by John Douglas and Mark Olshaker

1996

    Journey into Darkness by John Douglas and Mark
        Olshaker
    Angela's Ashes by Frank McCourt

1997

    Underworld by Don DeLillo
    The Joy of Cooking by Irma S. Rombauer, Marion
        Rombauer Becker, and Ethan Becker

1998

    Bag of Bones by Stephen King
    Bunts by George Will

❧ THE FREE PRESS

1986

The Morning After: American Successes and Excesses, 1981–1986 by George F. Will

1989

The Tempting of America by Robert H. Bork

1990

Suddenly by George F. Will

1991

A Question of Character: A Life of John F. Kennedy by Thomas C. Reeves

1992

The End of History and the Last Man by Francis Fukuyama

1993

The Real Anita Hill by David Brock

1994

The Bell Curve by Richard J. Hernnstein and Charles Murray

1997

Spin Cycle by Howard Kurtz

1998

The Death of Outrage by William J. Bennett

❧ SUMMIT

1978

The Women's Room by Marilyn French

1979

The Great Shark Hunt by Hunter S. Thompson

1980

    The Bleeding Heart by Marilyn French

1981

    The Cinderella Complex: Women's Hidden Fear of Independence by
        Colette Dowling
    Paper Money by Adam Smith

1982

    No Bad Dogs: The Woodhouse Way by Barbara Woodhouse

1983

    The Price of Power by Seymour M. Hersh

1984

    The Kennedys: An American Drama by Peter Collier and David
        Horowitz
    Heritage: Civilization and the Jews by Abba Eban

1986

    When All You've Ever Wanted Isn't Enough by Rabbi Harold S.
        Kushner
    The Man Who Mistook His Wife for a Hat and Other Clinical Tales by
        Oliver Sacks

1987

    And a Voice to Sing With by Joan Baez

1988

    *Generation of Swine: Tales of Shame and Degradation in the '80s: The
        Gonzo Papers, Vol. II* by Hunter S. Thompson

1989

    The Fortune by Michael Korda

1990

    Simone de Beauvoir by Deidre Bair
    Who Needs God? by Rabbi Harold S. Kushner

1992

    Awaken the Giant Within by Anthony Robbins

❧ LINDEN

1980

The Old Neighborhood by Avery Corman

1981

Second Opinion: Your Medical Alternatives by Isadore Rosenfeld, M.D.

1982

The Prodigal Daughter by Jeffrey Archer
Having It All by Helen Gurley Brown
The Invisible Bankers by Andrew Tobias

1984

First Among Equals by Jeffrey Archer
Men: An Owner's Manual by Stephanie Brush
Powerplay by Mary Cunningham with Fran Schumer

1985

Queenie by Michael Korda
The Sicilian by Mario Puzo
Last Wish by Betty Rollin

1986

A Matter of Honor by Jeffrey Archer
Modern Prevention: The New Medicine by Isadore Rosenfeld, M.D.

1987

The Jesuits by Malachi Martin

❧ POSEIDON

1982

Deceptions by Judith Michael

1984

Silver Wings, Santiago Blue by Janet Dailey
Possessions by Judith Michael

1986
> *The Great Alone* by Janet Dailey
> *Private Affairs* by Judith Michael

1988
> *Inheritance* by Judith Michael

1990
> *A Ruling Passion* by Judith Michael

1991
> *Sleeping Beauty* by Judith Michael

1993
> *Pot of Gold* by Judith Michael

1994
> *A Tangled Web* by Judith Michael

~ WYNDHAM

1980
> *Green Monday* by Michael M. Thomas

~ CHARLES SCRIBNER'S SONS, MACMILLAN, ATHENEUM

1919
> *Saint's Progress* by John Galsworthy (S)
> *Theodore Roosevelt's Letters to His Children*, Joseph Bucklin Bishop, ed. (S)
> *Mary Olivier* by May Sinclair (M)
> *The Valley of Vision* by Henry Van Dyke (S)
> *What Happened to Europe* by Frank A. Vanderlip (M)
> *The Undying Fire* by Herbert George Wells (M)

Charles Scribner's Sons, Macmillan, Atheneum bestsellers, continued

1920

Theodore Roosevelt and His Time, Shown in His Letters, 2 Vols.,
Joseph Bucklin Bishop, ed. (S)
This Side of Paradise by F. Scott Fitzgerald (S)
Erskine Dale, Pioneer by John Fox, Jr. (S)
Tatterdemalion by John Galsworthy (S)
Black Sheep! Black Sheep! by Meredith Nicholson (S)
A Straight Deal or the Ancient Grudge by Owen Wister (M)

1921

In Chancery by John Galsworthy (S)
Steeplejack by James G. Huneker (S)
The Outline of History by Herbert George Wells (M)

1922

The Americanization of Edward Bok by Edward W. Bok (S)
My Memories of Eighty Years by Chauncey M. Depew (S)
The Beautiful and the Damned by F. Scott Fitzgerald (S)
Maria Chapdelaine by Louis Hemon (M)
My Brother Theodore Roosevelt by Corinne Roosevelt Robinson (S)
Revolt Against Civilization by Lothrop Stoddard (S)
Secret Places of the Heart by Herbert George Wells (M)

1923

A Man from Maine by Edward W. Bok (S)
His Children's Children by Arthur Train (S)
A Short History of the World by H. G. Wells (M)
Men Like Gods by H. G. Wells (M)
A Son at the Front by Edith Wharton (S)

1924

Interpreter's House by Maxwell Struthers Burt (S)

1925

Twice Thirty by Edward W. Bok (S)
Drums by James Boyd (S)

Modern Use of the Bible by Harry Emerson Fosdick (M)
The White Monkey by John Galsworthy (S)

1926

This Believing World by Lewis Browne (M)
The Silver Spoon by John Galsworthy (S)
Our Times, 1909–1914 by Mark Sullivan (S)
Fix Bayonets! by Col. John W. Thomason, Jr., U.S.M.C. (S)

1927

Dawn by Irving Bacheller (M)
Marching On by James Boyd (S)
The Delectable Mountain by Maxwell Struthers Burt (S)
Your Money's Worth by Stuart Chase and F. J. Schlink (S)
Tristram by Edwin Arlington Robinson (M)
Our Times, Vol. 2, by Mark Sullivan (S)

1928

Swan Song by John Galsworthy (S)
My Autobiography by Benito Mussolini (S)
The Greene Murder Case by S. S. Van Dine (S)

1929

Men and Machines by Stuart Chase (M)
A Farewell to Arms by Ernest Hemingway (S)
A Preface to Morals by Walter Lippmann (M)
Cavender's House by Edwin Arlington Robinson (M)
The Bishop Murder Case by S. S. Van Dine (S)

1930

The Rise of American Civilization by Charles Austin Beard and
    Mary R. Beard (M)
On Forsyte 'Change by John Galsworthy (S)
Smokey, the Cowhorse by Will James (S)
Lone Cowboy by Will James (S)
The Universe Around Us by Sir James Jeans (M)
The Blacksmith of Vilno by Eric Philbrook Kelly (M)
The Trumpeter of Krakow by Eric Philbrook Kelly (M)

Charles Scribner's Sons, Macmillan, Atheneum bestsellers, continued

Mary Baker Eddy by Lyman P. Powell (M)
Pre-War America by Mark Sullivan (S)
The Scarab Murder Case by S. S. Van Dine (S)
Roosevelt, The Story of a Friendship by Owen Wister (M)

1931

Festival by Maxwell Struthers Burt (S)
Mexico by Stuart Chase (M)
The Cat Who Went to Heaven by Elizabeth Coatsworth (M)
Maid in Waiting by John Galsworthy (S)
The Farmer in the Dell by Berta Hader and Elmer Hader (M)
Sun-Up by Will James (S)
Big Enough by Will James (S)

1932

The March of Democracy by James Truslow Adams (S)
A New Deal by Stuart Chase (M)
The Story of My Life by Clarence Darrow (S)
Death in the Afternoon by Ernest Hemingway (S)

1933

The March of Democracy, Vol. 2, by James Truslow Adams (S)
Inheritance by Phyllis Eleanor Bentley (M)
As the Earth Turns by Gladys Hasty Carroll (M)
Flowering Wilderness by John Galsworthy (S)
One More River by John Galsworthy (S)
Winner Take Nothing by Ernest Hemingway (S)
South Moon Under by Marjorie Kinnan Rawlings (S)
The Kennel Murder Case by S. S. Van Dine (S)
The Bulpington of Blup by H. G. Wells (M)

1934

America's Tragedy by James Truslow Adams (S)
A Modern Tragedy by Phyllis Eleanor Bentley (M)
Testament of Youth by Vera Brittain (M)
Mary Peters by Mary Ellen Chase (M)

The Economy of Abundance by Stuart Chase (M)
Tender Is the Night by F. Scott Fitzgerald (S)
Brazilian Adventure by Peter Fleming (S)
The Challenge to Liberty by Herbert C. Hoover (S)
Full Flavour by Doris Leslie (M)
Crowded Hours by Alice Roosevelt Longworth (S)
The Bird of Dawning by John Masefield (M)
Over Here by Mark Sullivan (S)
Experiment in Autobiography by H. G. Wells (M)
So Red the Rose by Stark Young (S)

1935

Europa by Robert Briffault (S)
A Few Foolish Ones by Gladys Hasty Carroll (M)
Time Out of Mind by Rachel Field (M)
R. E. Lee by Douglas Southall Freeman (S)
Young Cowboy by Will James (S)
Golden Apples by Marjorie Kinnan Rawlings (S)
The Twenties by Mark Sullivan (S)
Of Time and the River by Thomas Wolfe (S)

1936

The Living Jefferson by James Truslow Adams (S)
Silas Crockett by Mary Ellen Chase (M)
Of Lena Geyer by Marcia Davenport (S)
Heads and Tales by Malvina Hoffman (S)
South Riding by Winifred Holtby (M)
Victorious Troy by John Masefield (M)
Gone with the Wind by Margaret Mitchell (M)
Sparkenbroke by Charles Morgan (M)
The Last Puritan by George Santayana (S)
The Rolling Years by Agnes Sligh Turnbull (M)

1937

We or They: Two Worlds in Conflict by Hamilton Fish Armstrong (M)
The Birds of America by John James Audubon (M)
Europa in Limbo by Robert Briffault (S)

Charles Scribner's Sons, Macmillan, Atheneum bestsellers, continued

Honourable Estate by Vera Brittain (M)
Neighbor to the Sky by Gladys Hasty Carroll (M)
To Have and Have Not by Ernest Hemingway (S)
The Return to Religion by Henry Charles Link (M)
Victoria 4:30 by Cecil Roberts (M)
And So—Victoria by Vaughan Wilkins (M)

1938

Fanny Kemble by Margaret Armstrong (M)
Sleep in Peace by Phyllis Eleanor Bentley (M)
Dynasty of Death by Taylor Caldwell (S)
Dawn in Lyonesse by Mary Ellen Chase (M)
A Southerner Discovers the South by Jonathan Daniels (M)
All This, and Heaven Too by Rachel Field (M)
Concord in Jeopardy by Doris Leslie (M)
The Rediscovery of Man by Henry Charles Link (M)
The Paderewski Memoirs by Ignace Jan Paderewski and Mary
  Lawton (S)
The Yearling by Marjorie Kinnan Rawlings (S)
A New Birth of Freedom by Nicholas Roosevelt (S)

1939

When There Is No Peace by Hamilton Fish Armstrong (M)
America in Midpassage by Charles Austin Beard and Mary R.
  Beard (M)
The Land Is Bright by Archie Binns (S)
Bitter Creek by James Boyd (S)
A Goodly Fellowship by Mary Ellen Chase (M)
Next to Valour by John Edward Jennings (M)
Frost and Fire by Elliott Merrick (S)
Wine of Good Hope by David Rame (M)
They Wanted to Live by Cecil Roberts (M)
Abe Lincoln in Illinois by Robert Emmet Sherwood (S)
The Woman in the Hall by Gladys Bronwyn Stern (M)
Maud by Richard L. Strout (M)

Remember the End by Agnes Sligh Turnbull (M)
A Puritan in Babylon by William Allen White (M)

1940

A Southerner Discovers New England by Jonathan Daniels (M)
For Whom the Bell Tolls by Ernest Hemingway (S)
How Green Was My Valley by Richard Llewellyn (M)
The Voyage by Charles Morgan (M)

1941

Trelawny by Margaret Armstrong (M)
They Came to a River by Allis McKay (M)

1942

Along These Streets by Maxwell Struthers Burt (S)
Windswept by Mary Ellen Chase (M)
Drivin' Woman by Elizabeth Pickett Chevalier (M)
The Valley of Decision by Marcia Davenport (S)
And Now Tomorrow by Rachel Field (M)
Lee's Lieutenants, Vol. 1, by Douglas Southall Freeman (S)
The Prodigal Women by Nancy Hale (S)
The Long Ships Passing by Walter Havighurst (M)
Only One Storm by Granville Hicks (M)
With Japan's Leaders by Frederick Moore (S)
Cross Creek by Marjorie Kinnan Rawlings (S)
One Small Candle by Cecil Roberts (M)
The Day Must Dawn by Agnes Sligh Turnbull (M)

1943

Social Insurance and Allied Services by Sir William Henry Beveridge
    (M)
Mr. Justice Holmes by Francis Biddle (S)
The Arm and the Darkness by Taylor Caldwell (S)
Harriet by Florence Ryerson Clements and Colin Clements (S)
Lee's Lieutenants, Vol. 2, by Douglas Southall Freeman (S)
Tomorrow the World by James Gow and Armand d'Usseau (S)
Our Way Down East by Elinor Graham (M)
None but the Lonely Heart by Richard Llewellyn (M)

Charles Scribner's Sons, Macmillan, Atheneum bestsellers, continued

The Choice by Charles Mills (M)
The Legacy of Nazism by Frank Munk (M)
Headhunting in the Solomon Islands by Caroline Mytinger (M)
The Spirit of Enterprise by Edgar Monsanto Queeny (S)
God Is My Co-Pilot by Col. Robert L. Scott, Jr. (S)
Hope Deferred by Jeanette Seletz (M)
Paris Underground by Etta Shiber (S)
The Three Bamboos by Robert Standish (M)
The Young Matriarch by Gladys Bronwyn Stern (M)
Moment of Truth by Col. Charles Sweeny (S)
And a Few Marines by Col. John W. Thomason, Jr., U.S.M.C. (S)
Yankee Lawyer: The Autobiography of Ephraim Tutt by Ephraim Tutt
    (S)
Only the Valiant by Charles Marquis Warren (M)
We Cannot Escape History by John Thompson Whitaker (M)

1944

Album of American History by James Truslow Adams (S)
The Final Hour by Taylor Caldwell (S)
Lee's Lieutenants, Vol. 3, by Douglas Southall Freeman (S)
The Red Cock Crows by Frances Gaither (M)
Liana by Martha Gellhorn (S)
Men of Maryknoll by James Keller and Meyer Berger (S)
The History of Rome Hanks by Joseph Stanley Pennell (S)
Persons and Places by George Santayana (S)
Bonin by Robert Standish (M)
Lend-Lease: Weapon for Victory by Edward Reilly Stettinius, Jr. (M)
Indigo by Christine Weston (S)
Being Met Together by Vaughan Wilkins (M)
Forever Amber by Kathleen Winsor (M)

1945

American Chronicle by Ray Stannard Baker (S)
Buffalo Coat by Carol Brink (M)
The Wide House by Taylor Caldwell (S)

Teresa: Or Her Demon Lover by Austin Kayingham Gray (S)
A Guide for the Bedevilled by Ben Hecht (S)
Pride's Way by Robert Molloy (M)
Fighting Liberal by George William Norris (M)
The Middle Span by George Santayana (S)
Put Off Thy Shoes by Ethel Lillian Boole Voynich (M)

1946

Do I Wake or Sleep? by Isabel Bolton (S)
The Great Globe Itself by William C. Bullitt (S)
This Side of Innocence by Taylor Caldwell (S)
The First Freedom by Morris Leopold Ernst (M)
George Washington, Vols. 1 & 2, by Douglas Southall Freeman (S)
Mademoiselle's Home Planning Scrapbook by Elinor Hillyer (M)
Thieves in the Night by Arthur Koestler (M)
I Chose Freedom by Victor Kravchenko (S)
Singing Waters by Mary Dolling Sanders O'Malley (M)
Fanfare for Elizabeth by Dame Edith Sitwell (M)
The Autobiography of William Allen White by William Allen White (M)
The Dark Wood by Christine Wood (S)

1947

There Was a Time by Taylor Caldwell (S)
East Side, West Side by Marcia Davenport (S)
Journey to the End of an Era by Melvin Adams Hall (S)
Spring in Washington by Louis Joseph Halle (A)
Holdfast Gaines by Odell Shepard and Willard Shepard (M)
The Last Days of Hitler by H. R. Trevor-Roper (M)

1948

The Tamarack by Howard Breslin (M)
Melissa by Taylor Caldwell (S)
The Memoirs of Cordell Hull by Cordell Hull (M)
The Flames of Time by Baynard Hardwick Kendrick (S)
Of Flight and Life by Col. Charles A. Lindbergh (S)
The Inside Story of the Pendergast Machine by Maurice M. Milligan (S)
Cry, the Beloved Country by Alan Paton (S)

Charles Scribner's Sons, Macmillan, Atheneum bestsellers, continued

The Last Billionaire by William C. Richards (S)
The Burnished Blade by Lawrence L. Schoonover (M)
The Bishop's Mantle by Agnes Sligh Turnbull (M)
Age of the Great Depression, 1929–1941 by Dison Wecter (M)

1949

Hunter's Horn by Harriette Louisa Simpson Arnow (M)
Let Love Come Last by Taylor Caldwell (S)
West of the Hill by Gladys Hasty Carroll (M)
Double Muscadine by Frances Gaither (M)
Alcatraz Island Prison by James A. Johnston (S)
The Golden Warrior by Hope Muntz (S)
Coral and Brass by Holland McTyeire Smith and Percy Finch (S)
Elephant Walk by Robert Standish (M)

1950

Information Please Almanac 1950 (M)
The Strange Land by Ned Calmer (S)
War or Peace by John Foster Dulles (M)
The Sign of Jonah by Nancy Hale (S)
Across the River and into the Trees by Ernest Hemingway (S)
The Backward Bride by Salvator Aubrey Clarence Menen (S)
Worlds in Collision by Immanuel Velikovsky (M)

1951

Tito and Goliath by Hamilton Fish Armstrong (M)
The Balance Wheel by Taylor Caldwell (S)
George Washington, Vols. 3 & 4, by Douglas Southall Freeman (S)
The Memoirs of Herbert Hoover by Herbert C. Hoover (M)
From Here to Eternity by James Jones (S)
Fifty Billion Dollars by Jesse H. Jones and Edward Angly (M)
The Age of Longing by Arthur Koestler (M)
Rain on the Wind by Walter Macken (M)
The Antoinette Pope School Cook Book by Antoinette Pope (M)
Dominations and Powers by George Santayana (S)

Jenkin's Ear by Odell Shepard and Willard Shepard (M)
The Foundling by Cardinal Francis Joseph Spellman (S)

1952

SPQR by Paul Hyde Bonner (S)
The Old Man and the Sea by Ernest Hemingway (S)
The Memoirs of Herbert Hoover, Vol. 2, by Herbert C. Hoover (M)
The Memoirs of Herbert Hoover, Vol. 3, by Herbert C. Hoover (M)
Postmarked Moscow by Lydia Kirk (S)
The Duke of Gallodoro by Salvator Aubrey Clarence Menen (S)
The Dark Moment by Mary Dolling Sanders O'Malley (M)
The Man on a Donkey by Hilda Frances Margaret Prescott (M)

1953

Hotel Talleyrand by Paul Hyde Bonner (S)
Divided We Fought by David Herbert Donald (M)
The Spirit of St. Louis by Col. Charles A. Lindbergh (S)
Too Late the Phalarope by Alan Paton (S)
The Sojourner by Marjorie Kinnan Rawlings (S)
My Host the World by George Santayana (S)

1954

The Dollmaker by Harriette Louisa Simpson Arnow (M)
My Brother's Keeper by Marcia Davenport (S)
The Roosevelt Family of Sagamore Hill by Hermann Hagedorn (M)
The Ramayana as told by Salvator Aubrey Clarence Menen (S)
The Spider King by Lawrence L. Schoonover (M)
Not as a Stranger by Morton Thompson (S)

1955

Excelsior! by Paul Hyde Bonner (S)
The Thanksgiving Story by Alice Dalgliesh (S)
A Dream of Kings by Davis Grubb (S)

1956

With Both Eyes Open by Paul Hyde Bonner (S)
The Abode of Love by Salvator Aubrey Clarence Menen (S)
Sickles the Incredible by W. A. Swanberg (S)

Charles Scribner's Sons, Macmillan, Atheneum bestsellers, continued

1957

Never So Few by Tom T. Chamales (S)
The Last Angry Man by Gerald Green (S)
Challenge to Venus by Charles Morgan (M)
The Philadelphian by Richard Powell (S)

1958

Some Came Running by James Jones (S)
The Portuguese Escape by Mary Dolling Sanders O'Malley (M)
The New Testament in Modern English, trans. by J. B. Phillips (M)

1959

The Art of Llewellyn Jones by Paul Hyde Bonner (S)
The Lotus Eaters by Gerald Green (S)
The Watch That Ends the Night by Hugh MacLennan (S)
The Fig Tree by Salvator Aubrey Clarence Menen (S)
Pioneer, Go Home! by Richard Powell (S)
This Is Paris by Miroslav Sasek (M)
The Elements of Style by William Strunk, Jr., and E. B. White (M)
The Thirteenth Apostle by Eugene Vale (S)

1960

The Constant Image by Marcia Davenport (S)
The Inspector by Jan de Hartog (A)
The Wind in the Willows by Kenneth Grahame (S)
A Separate Peace by John Knowles (M)
Kennedy or Nixon: Does It Matter? by Arthur M. Schlesinger, Jr.
(M)
The Last of the Just by Andre Schwarz-Bart (A)
The Affair by C. P. Snow (S)

1961

The Heartless Light by Gerald Green (S)
Tales from a Troubled Land by Alan Paton (S)
A Matter of Life and Death by Virgilia Peterson (A)
This Is New York by Miroslav Sasek (M)

Citizen Hearst by W. A. Swanberg (S)
The Making of the President, 1960 by Theodore H. White (A)

1962

Thumbelina by Hans Christian Andersen (S)
One Man's Freedom by Edward Bennett (A)
Once a Mouse . . . by Marcia Brown (S)
O Ye Jigs & Juleps! by Virginia Cary (M)
Christopher of San Francisco by George Dorsey (M)
The Lattimer Legend by Ann Hebson (M)
The Thin Red Line by James Jones (S)
The Forgotten Smile by Margaret Kennedy (M)
The Rothschilds by Frederic Morton (A)
A Long and Happy Life by Reynolds Price (A)
This Is San Francisco by Miroslav Sasek (M)
Act of Anger by Bart Spicer (A)
The Guns of August by Barbara W. Tuchman (M)
Scott Fitzgerald by Andrew Turnbull (S)

1963

The Ordeal of Power by Emmet John Hughes (A)
JFK: The Man and the Myth by Victor Lasky (M)
I Take This Land by Richard Powell (S)
The Bedford Incident by Mark Rascovich (A)
The Margaret Rudkin Pepperidge Farm Cookbook by Margaret Rudkin (A)
John F. Kennedy by Hugh Sidey (A)
The Letters of F. Scott Fitzgerald, Andrew Turnbull, ed. (S)

1964

A Kind of Anger by Eric Ambler (A)
A Moveable Feast by Ernest Hemingway (S)
Sixpence in Her Shoe by Phyllis McGinley (M)
Confessions of an Advertising Man by David Ogilvy (A)
My Favorite Things by Dorothy Rodgers (A)

1965

The Italians by Luigi Barzini (A)
A Covenant with Death by Stephen Becker (A)

Charles Scribner's Sons, Macmillan, Atheneum bestsellers, continued

Manchild in the Promised Land by Claude Brown (M)
May I Bring a Friend? by Beatrice Schenk De Regniers (A)
Midnight Plus One by Gavin Lyall (S)
Taken Care Of: The Autobiography of Edith Sitwell by Dame Edith
   Sitwell (A)
The Making of the President, 1964 by Theodore H. White (A)

1966

The Territorial Imperative by Robert Ardrey (A)
Tai-Pan by James Clavell (A)
Shogun by James Clavell (A)
The Secular City by Harvey G. Cox (M)
A Generous Man by Reynolds Price (A)
The Proud Tower by Barbara W. Tuchman (M)

1967

A Night of Watching by Elliott Arnold (S)
Too Strong for Fantasy by Marcia Davenport (S)
The Captain by Jan de Hartog (A)
Nicholas and Alexandra by Robert K. Massie (A)
Harold Nicolson's Diaries and Letters, 1930–1939, Nigel Nicolson,
   ed. (A)
Harold Nicolson: The War Years 1939–1945, Nigel Nicolson,
   ed. (A)
Variety of Men by C. P. Snow (S)
By-Line: Ernest Hemingway, William White, ed. (S)

1968

A Mass for the Dead by William Gibson (A)
Between Parent and Child by Dr. Haim G. Ginott (M)
Harold Nicolson: The Later Years 1945–1962, Nigel Nicolson, ed.
   (A)
The American Challenge by Jean-Jacques Servan-Schreiber (A)
Thomas Wolfe by Andrew Turnbull (S)
The Double Helix by James D. Watson (A)

1969

Ernest Hemingway: A Life Story by Carlos Baker (S)
Between Parent and Teenager by Dr. Haim G. Ginott (M)
The Sleep of Reason by C. P. Snow (S)
A Long Row of Candles by C. L. Sulzberger (M)
The Making of the President, 1968 by Theodore H. White (A)

1970

Islands in the Stream by Ernest Hemingway (S)
Inside the Third Reich by Albert Speer (M)

1971

Tarantula by Bob Dylan (M)
Myself Among Others by Ruth Gordon (A)
Stilwell and the American Experience in China 1911–1945 by Barbara
   W. Tuchman (S)

1972

The Levanter by Eric Ambler (A)
Jonathan Livingston Seagull by Richard Bach (M)
Semi-Tough by Dan Jenkins (A)
Luce and His Empire by W. A. Swanberg (S)
George S. Kaufman: An Intimate Portrait by Howard M. Teichmann
   (A)

1973

The Billion-Dollar Sure Thing by Paul E. Erdman (S)
Portrait of a Marriage by Nigel Nicolson (A)
The Making of the President, 1972 by Theodore H. White (A)

1974

Watership Down by Richard Adams (M)
The Silver Bears by Paul E. Erdman (S)
The Great Gatsby by F. Scott Fitzgerald (S)
128 House Plants You Can Grow by Ron Herwig (M)
128 More House Plants You Can Grow by Ron Herwig (M)
An American Life by Jeb Stuart Magruder (A)

Charles Scribner's Sons, Macmillan, Atheneum bestsellers, continued

1976
> *Spandau: The Secret Diaries* by Albert Speer (M)
> *Sinatra* by Earl Wilson (M)

1977
> *The Hite Report: A Nationwide Study of Female Sexuality* by Shere Hite (M)
> *On Death and Dying* by Elisabeth Kubler-Ross, M.D. (M)
> *East Wind, Rain* by N. Richard Nash (A)
> *The Cracker Factory* by Joyce Rebeta-Burditt (M)

1978
> *Adrien Arpel's Three-Week Crash Makeover/Shapeover Beauty Program* by Adrien Arpel with Ronnie Sue Ebenstein (A)
> *The Last Magic* by N. Richard Nash (A)

1979
> *The Third World War: August 1985* by Gen. Sir John Hackett (M)
> *The Vicar of Christ* by Walter F. Murphy (M)
> *The Non-Runner's Book* by Vic Ziegel and Lewis Grossberger (M)

1980
> *How to Look Ten Years Younger* by Adrien Arpel with Ronnie Sue Ebenstein (Rawson Wade/Atheneum)
> *Good Morning, Merry Sunshine: A Father's Journal of His Child's First Year* by Bob Greene (A)
> *Innocent Blood* by P. D. James (S)

1981
> *Best Evidence* by David S. Lifton (M)
> *The Beverly Hills Diet* by Judy Mazel (M)
> *A Few Minutes with Andy Rooney* by Andy Rooney (A)

1982
> *Happy to Be Here* by Garrison Keillor (A)
> *Miss Manners' Guide to Excruciatingly Correct Behavior* by Judith Martin (A)
> *And More by Andy Rooney* by Andy Rooney (A)

1983

Royal Service by Stephen P. Barry (M)
A Hero for Our Time by Ralph G. Martin (M)

1984

Caveat: Realism, Reagan and Foreign Policy by Alexander M. Haig,
   Jr. (M)
The Journeyer by Gary Jennings (A)
Miss Manners' Guide to Rearing Perfect Children by Judith Martin (A)
Pieces of My Mind by Andy Rooney (A)

1985

At Mother's Request by Jonathan Coleman (A)
The Dangerous Summer by Ernest Hemingway (S)
Goddess: The Secret Lives of Marilyn Monroe by Anthony Summers
   (M)

1986

Stranger in Two Worlds by Jean Harris (M)
The Garden of Eden by Ernest Hemingway (S)
Arctic Dreams by Barry Lopez *(S)*
Gone with the Wind Fiftieth Anniversary Facsimile Edition by Margaret
   Mitchell (M)
Kate Vaiden by Reynolds Price (A)
Bess W. Truman by Margaret Truman (M)

1987

A Season on the Brink by John Feinstein (M)
Be True to Your School by Bob Greene (A)

1988

Speaking Out: The Reagan Presidency from Inside the White House by
   Larry Speakes and Robert Pack (S)

1989

Grand Failure: Communism's Terminal Crisis by Zbigniew Brzezinski
   (S)
Joshua and the Children by Joseph F. Girzone (M)
Pete Rose: My Story by Pete Rose and Roger Kahn (M)

Charles Scribner's Sons, Macmillan, Atheneum bestsellers, continued

1990

The Shepherd by Joseph F. Girzone (M)
Mere Christianity by C. S. Lewis (M)
Captain Sir Richard Francis Burton by Edward Rice (S)
Men at Work by George F. Will (M)

1992

All That Remains by Patricia Cornwell (S)
Two Nations: Black & White, Separate, Hostile, Unequal by Andrew
    Hacker (S)

1993

Cruel & Unusual by Patricia Cornwell (S)
Kaffir Boy in America: An Encounter with Apartheid by Mark
    Mathabane (S)
Turmoil & Triumph by George P. Shultz (S)

POCKET BOOKS BESTSELLERS*

~ POCKET BOOKS—PAPERBACKS

1974

In One Era and Out the Other by Sam Levenson
The Salamander by Morris L. West

1975

Give Us This Day by R. F. Delderfield
The Bottom Line by Fletcher Knebel
The Total Woman by Marabel Morgan
The Pirate by Harold Robbins

1976

Secrets by Burt Hirschfeld

1977

The Company by John D. Ehrlichman
Washington Behind Closed Doors by John D. Ehrlichman
The Crash of '79 by Paul E. Erdman
Everything You've Always Wanted to Know About Energy but Were Too Weak to Ask by Nora Hayden
79 Park Avenue by Harold Robbins
The Lonely Lady by Harold Robbins
Purity's Passion by Janette Seymour
A Fire in the Blood by Mary Kay Simmons

*List compiled from the *New York Times* paperback list since its beginning in 1967 and *Publishers Weekly* paperback and mass-market lists since their inception in 1976.

Pocket Books paperback bestsellers, continued

1978

Loose Change by Sara Davidson
The Betsy by Harold Robbins
Dreams Die First by Harold Robbins
The Word by Irving Wallace

1979

Flowers in the Attic by V. C. Andrews
Adrien Arpel's Three-Week Crash Makeover/Shapeover Beauty Program
    by Adrien Arpel with Ronnie Sue Ebenstein (Wallaby)
Wifey by Judy Blume
Touch the Wind by Janet Dailey
Love Kills by Dan Greenburg
The World According to Garp by John Irving
Laurel Canyon by Steve Krantz
The Passing Bells by Phillip Rock (Seaview)
Star Trek: The Novel by Gene Roddenberry

1980

Petals on the Wind by V. C. Andrews
The Rogue by Janet Dailey
Ride the Thunder by Janet Dailey
The Year of the French by Thomas Flanagan
Moviola by Garson Kanin
Maggie by Lena Kennedy
The Pope of Greenwich Village by Vincent Patrick
Memories of Another Day by Harold Robbins
Ghost Story by Peter Straub
First Strike by Douglas Terman
War and Remembrance by Herman Wouk

1981

If There Be Thorns by V. C. Andrews
Night Way by Janet Dailey
This Calder Sky by Janet Dailey

Whip Hand by Dick Francis
Kitty by Lena Kennedy
Heartsounds by Martha Weinman Lear
The Cat's Revenge by Philip Lief (Wallaby)
Emmeline by Judith Rossner
The I-Hate-Preppies Handbook by Ralph Schoenstein (Wallaby)

1982

666 by Jay Anson
This Calder Range by Janet Dailey
The Cinderella Complex: Women's Hidden Fear of Independence by
    Colette Dowling
Dutch Shea, Jr. by John Gregory Dunne
How to Win at Pac-Man by the Editors of *Consumer Guide*
The Last Days of America by Paul E. Erdman
Real Men Don't Eat Quiche by Bruce Feirstein
The Official M.B.A. Handbook by Jim Fisk and Robert Barron
    (Wallaby)
The Wrath of Kahn by Vonda N. McIntyre
Wild Honey by Fern Michaels
Goodbye, Janette by Harold Robbins
The Hunger by Whitley Strieber
The Best of Dear Abby by Abigail Van Buren

1983

Life, the Universe and Everything by Douglas Adams
The Hitchhiker's Guide to the Galaxy by Douglas Adams
My Sweet Audrina by V. C. Andrews
The Prodigal Daughter by Jeffrey Archer
Having It All by Helen Gurley Brown
Lace by Shirley Conran
Yesterday's Son by A. C. Crispin
Stands a Calder Man by Janet Dailey
Calder Born, Calder Bred by Janet Dailey
Velvet Song by Jude Deveraux
Linda Evans' Beauty and Exercise Book by Linda Evans (Wallaby)
Real Women Don't Pump Gas by Joyce Jillson

Pocket Books paperback bestsellers, continued

Deceptions by Judith Michael
Real Men Don't Cook Quiche by Scott Redman and Bruce Feirstein
Spellbinder by Harold Robbins
The Color Purple by Alice Walker (Washington Square)

1984

Seeds of Yesterday by V. C. Andrews
Hollywood Wives by Jackie Collins
The World Is Full of Married Men by Jackie Collins
Sinners by Jackie Collins
The Bitch by Jackie Collins
Heartburn by Nora Ephron
Winter's Tale by Mark Helprin
Fortunes by Barney Leason
The Vulcan Academy Murders by Jean Lorrah
The Search for Spock by Vonda N. McIntyre
Monimbo by Robert Moss and Arnaud de Borchgrave
Morning Glory by Julia Cleaver Smith
Jane's House by Robert Kimmel Smith
The Tears of the Singers by Melinda Snodgrass
Seeds of Greatness by Denis Waitley
The Official Lawyer's Handbook by D. Robert White (Wallaby)

1985

So Long, and Thanks for All the Fish by Douglas Adams
Heaven by V. C. Andrews
First Among Equals by Jeffrey Archer
Smart Women by Judy Blume
Dwellers in the Crucible by Margaret Wander Bonanno
Lace II by Shirley Conran
Deep Six by Clive Cussler
Silver Wings, Santiago Blue by Janet Dailey
The Pride of Hannah Wade by Janet Dailey
The Living Heart Diet by Michael E. DeBakey, M.D.; Antonio M.
     Gotto, Jr.; Lynne W. Scott; and John P. Foreyt (Raven)

Counterfeit Lady by Jude Deveraux
Twin of Fire by Jude Deveraux
Twin of Ice by Jude Deveraux
Lost Lady by Jude Deveraux
River Lady by Jude Deveraux
Possessions by Judith Michael
Machine Dreams by Jayne Anne Phillips
Descent from Xanadu by Harold Robbins
Lovesong by Valerie Sherwood
Killing Time by Della Van Hise
Wired: The Short Life and Fast Times of John Belushi by Bob
    Woodward

1986

Dark Angel by V. C. Andrews
Cops: Their Lives in Their Words by Mark Baker
Dreadnought by Diane Carey
Battlestations! by Diane Carey
Lucky by Jackie Collins
Cyclops by Clive Cussler
The Glory Game by Janet Dailey
The Temptress by Jude Deveraux
Demons by J. M. Dillard
Smart Cookies Don't Crumble by Sonya Friedman
J.K. Lasser's What the New Tax Law Means to You by J. K. Lasser
    Tax Institute
Bundy: The Deliberate Stranger by Richard W. Larsen
The Voyage Home by Vonda N. McIntyre
Enterprise: The First Adventure by Vonda N. McIntyre
Women Who Love Too Much by Robin Norwood
Windsong by Valerie Sherwood
The Titan by Fred Mustard Stewart

1987

Garden of Shadows by V. C. Andrews
A Matter of Honor by Jeffrey Archer
Strangers from the Sky by Margaret Wander Bonanno

143

Pocket Books paperback bestsellers, continued

Dreams of the Raven by Carmen Carter
Hollywood Husbands by Jackie Collins
Flight of the Intruder by Stephen Coonts
The Great Alone by Janet Dailey
The Raider by Jude Deveraux
The Princess by Jude Deveraux
Chain of Attack by Gene DeWeese
Bloodthirst by J. M. Dillard
The Romulan Way by Diane Duane and Peter Morwood
How Much for Just the Planet? by John M. Ford
Encounter at Farpoint by David Gerrold
Poor Little Rich Girl by C. David Heymann
Catmopolitan by Ilene Hochberg
When All You've Ever Wanted Isn't Enough by Rabbi Harold S. Kushner
Swan Song by Robert R. McCammon
Private Affairs by Judith Michael
Taking the Stand: The Testimony of Lieutenant Colonel Oliver L. North
    by Oliver L. North
Wiseguy: The Rise and Fall of a Mobster by Nicholas Pileggi
Amerika by Brauna E. Pouns
The Storyteller by Harold Robbins
Perfume by Patrick Suskind
Deep Domain by Howard Weinstein

1988

Dirk Gently's Holistic Detective Agency by Douglas Adams
Fallen Hearts by V. C. Andrews
Empire of the Sun by J. G. Ballard
Passion Moon Rising by Rebecca Brandewyne
Ghost Ship by Diane Carey
Final Frontier by Diane Carey
Rock Star by Jackie Collins
Savages by Shirley Conran
Time for Yesterday by A. C. Crispin

Treasure by Clive Cussler
The Maiden by Jude Deveraux
The Awakening by Jude Deveraux
Timetrap by David Dvorkin
The Final Nexus by Gene DeWeese
Wideacre by Philippa Gregory
Satisfaction by Rae Lawrence
The Idic Epidemic by Jean Lorrah
Stinger by Robert R. McCammon
Texasville by Larry McMurtry
Something Wonderful by Judith McNaught
The Three-Minute Universe by Barbara Paul
Memory Prime by Garfield Reeves-Stevens and Judith Reeves-Stevens
Reindeer Moon by Elizabeth Marshall Thomas
Veil: The Secret Wars of the CIA, 1981–1987 by Bob Woodward

1989

Gates of Paradise by V. C. Andrews
Prime Time by Joan Collins
Wishes by Jude Deveraux
The Taming by Jude Deveraux
The Final Frontier by J. M. Dillard
The Ragman's Son by Kirk Douglas
The Captain's Honor by David Dvorkin and Daniel Dvorkin
The Kobayashi Maru by Julia Ecklar
Vulcan's Glory by D. C. Fontana
Double, Double by Michael Jan Friedman
A Glimpse of Stocking by Elizabeth Gage
Gentle Warrior by Julie Garwood
The Bride by Julie Garwood
The Cry of the Onlies by Judy Klass
The Wolf's Hour by Robert R. McCammon
Lonesome Dove by Larry McMurtry
Anything for Billy by Larry McMurtry
A Kingdom of Dreams by Judith McNaught
The Crosskillers by Marcel Mantecino

145

Pocket Books paperback bestsellers, continued

Inheritance by Judith Michael
Fancy Pants by Susan Elizabeth Phillips
Masks by John Vornholt

1990

The Long Dark Tea-Time of the Soul by Douglas Adams
Dawn by V. C. Andrews
Web of Dreams by V. C. Andrews
A Twist in the Tale by Jeffrey Archer
Doomsday World by Carmen Carter with Peter David, Michael Jan
     Friedman, and Robert Greenberger
The Eyes of the Beholders by A. C. Crispin
A Rock and a Hard Place by Peter David
Too Deep for Tears by Kathryn Lynn Davis
Mountain Laurel by Jude Deveraux
Doctor's Orders by Diane Duane
Postcards from the Edge by Carrie Fisher
Fortune's Light by Michael Jan Friedman
The Gift by Julie Garwood
Honor's Splendour by Julie Garwood
Rebellious Desire by Julie Garwood
Guardian Angel by Julie Garwood
Trail of Lies by Carolyn Keene
Model Crime by Carolyn Keene
Born on the Fourth of July by Ron Kovic
Home Is the Hunter by Dana Kramer-Rolls
The Late Night with David Letterman Book of Top Ten Lists by David
     Letterman with Steve O'Donnell, et al.
Metamorphosis by Jean Lorrah
The Secret Diary of Laura Palmer by Jennifer Lynch
Some Can Whistle by Larry McMurtry
Buffalo Girls by Larry McMurtry
Almost Heaven by Judith McNaught
Lives and Loves of the New Kids on the Block by Jill Matthews

Enemy Unseen by V. E. Mitchell
Rules of Engagement by Peter Morwood
Witch by Christopher Pike
See You Later by Christopher Pike
Fall into Darkness by Christopher Pike
The Boyfriend by Christopher Pike
The Bridesmaids by Judith Balaban Quine
Gulliver's Fugitives by Keith Sharee
The Blessing by Gary Smalley and John Trent
The Stepsister by R. L. Stine
The Cuckoo's Egg: Tracking a Spy Through the Maze of Computer Espionage by Clifford Stoll
The Temple of My Familiar by Alice Walker

1991

Secrets of the Morning by V. C. Andrews
The Anastasia Syndrome and Other Stories by Mary Higgins Clark
Lady Boss by Jackie Collins
Under Siege by Stephen Coonts
Bright Star by Harold Coyle
Dragon by Clive Cussler
Q-in-Law by Peter David
The Rift by Peter David
Vendetta by Peter David
The Conquest by Jude Deveraux
Renegade by Gene Deweese
Star Trek VI: The Undiscovered Country by J. M. Dillard
A Flag Full of Stars by Brad Ferguson
Surrender the Pink by Carrie Fisher
Legacy by Michael Jan Friedman
The Prize by Julie Garwood
Boogeyman by Mel Gilden
The Ghost-Walker by Barbara Hambly
The Eagle Has Flown by Jack Higgins
Sweet Fortune by Jayne Ann Krentz
An Altogether New Book of Top Ten Lists by David Letterman

Pocket Books paperback bestsellers, continued

In a Child's Name by Peter Maas
Lonesome Dove by Larry McMurtry
A Ruling Passion by Judith Michael
Prime Directive by Judith and Garfield Reeves-Stevens
Going Home by Danielle Steel
Unification by Jeri Taylor
Contamination by John Vornholt
Perchance to Dream by Howard Weinstein

1992

Twilight's Child by V. C. Andrews
Midnight Whispers by V. C. Andrews
Loves Music, Loves to Dance by Mary Higgins Clark
The Last of the Mohicans by James Fenimore Cooper
The Disinherited by Peter David and Michael Jan Friedman
The Duchess by Jude Deveraux
Eternity by Jude Deveraux
Faces of Fire by Michael Jan Friedman
Relics by Michael Jan Friedman
The Secret by Julie Garwood
Death Count by L. A. Graf
Ice Trap by L. A. Graf
Nightshade by Laurell K. Hamilton
Nancy Reagan by Kitty Kelley
Family Man by Jayne Ann Krentz
Perfect Partners by Jayne Ann Krentz
A River Runs Through It by Norman Maclean
Spartacus by Mancour
Boy's Life by Robert R. McCammon
Cruel Doubt by Joe McGinniss
Chains of Command by W. A. McCay and E. L. Flood
Sleeping Beauty by Judith Michael
Daniel's Bride by Linda Miller
Imbalance by V. E. Mitchell

Diana: Her True Story by Andrew Morton
L.A. Secret Police by Mike Rothmiller
The Piranhas by Harold Robbins
If You Really Loved Me by Ann Rule
Sanctuary by John Vornholt
War Drums by John Vornholt

1993

Darkest Hour by V. C. Andrews
Grounded by David Bischoff
Best Destiny by Diane Carey
Descent by Diane Carey
The Great Starship Race by Diane Carey
The Devil's Heart by Carmen Carter
All Around the Town by Mary Higgins Clark
American Star by Jackie Collins
Sahara by Clive Cussler
Sweet Liar by Jude Deveraux
Dark Mirror by Diane Duane
Memories by Ralph Emery
Women on Top by Nancy Friday
Castles by Julie Garwood
Saving Grace by Julie Garwood
The First Wives Club by Olivia Goldsmith
The Romulan Prize by Simon Hawke
MTV's Beavis and Butt-head by Sam Johnson
Wildest Hearts by Jayne Ann Krentz
Hidden Talents by Jayne Ann Krentz
Disappearing Acts by Terry McMillan
Waiting to Exhale by Terry McMillan
Yankee Wife by Linda Lael Miller
Here There Be Dragons by John Peel
A Rose for Her Grave by Ann Rule
Everything She Ever Wanted by Ann Rule
The Silent Passage by Gail Sheehy
The Jordan Rules by Sam Smith

Pocket Books paperback bestsellers, continued

1994

Pearl in the Mist by V. C. Andrews
Ruby by V. C. Andrews
I'll Be Seeing You by Mary Higgins Clark
The Ten Thousand by Harold Coyle
The Invitation by Jude Deveraux
Prince Charming by Julie Garwood
Forrest Gump by Winston Groom
Gumpisms by Winston Groom
MTV's Beavis and Butt-head: This Book Sucks by Sam Johnson
Ensucklopedia/MTV's Beavis and Butt-head by Sam Johnson, Chris
     Marcil, et al.
Grand Passion by Jayne Ann Krentz
See, I Told You So by Rush Limbaugh
The Last Brother by Joe McGinniss
Streets of Laredo by Larry McMurtry
A Holiday of Love by Judith McNaught, Jude Deveraux, Jill
     Barnett, and Arnette Lamb
Pot of Gold by Judith Michael
Princess Annie by Linda Lael Miller
The Legacy by Linda Lael Miller
You Belong to Me by Ann Rule
Private Parts by Howard Stern
Debtor's Planet by W. R. Thompson

1995

Little Women by Louisa May Alcott
All That Glitters by V. C. Andrews
Hidden Jewel by V. C. Andrews
Remember Me by Mary Higgins Clark
The Lottery Winner by Mary Higgins Clark
Hollywood Kids by Jackie Collins
Inca Gold by Clive Cussler
The Heiress by Jude Deveraux

Remembrance by Jude Deveraux
Driven to Distraction by Edward M. Hallowell and John J. Ratey
After the Night by Linda Howard
Dream Man by Linda Howard
The Real Real World by Hillary Johnson and Nancy Rommelmann
Everlasting Love by Jayne Ann Krentz and Linda Lael Miller
Apollo 13 by Jim Lovell
The Hidden Life of Dogs by Elizabeth Marshall
A Tangled Web by Judith Michael
Selena! by Clint Richmond
The Agenda by Bob Woodward

1996

Tarnished Gold by V. C. Andrews
Melody by V. C. Andrews
Let Me Call You Sweetheart by Mary Higgins Clark
Silent Night by Mary Higgins Clark
Moonlight Becomes You by Mary Higgins Clark
My Gal Sunday by Mary Higgins Clark
Shock Wave by Clive Cussler
Mindhunter by John Douglas and Mark Olshaker
Shades of Twilight by Linda Howard
Dead Man's Walk by Larry McMurtry
Dead by Sunset by Ann Rule
A Fever in the Heart by Ann Rule

1997

Heart Song by V. C. Andrews
Unfinished Symphony by V. C. Andrews
The Sea Hunters by Clive Cussler and Craig Dirgo
New Frontier, Books 1–4, by Peter David
Journey into Darkness by John Douglas
Clayborne Brides by Julie Garwood
Son of the Morning by Linda Howard
Kill and Tell by Linda Howard
She's Come Undone by Wally Lamb
Hanson by Jill Matthews

Pocket Books paperback bestsellers, continued

Diana: Her New Life by Andrew Morton
Prince William: The Boy Who Will Be King by Randi Reisfield
In the Name of Love by Ann Rule
Contact by Carl Sagan
The Decline and Fall of the House of Windsor by Donald Spoto

1998

Music in the Night by V. C. Andrews
Orphans: Butterfly, Crystal, Brooke and Raven by V. C. Andrews
Runaways by V. C. Andrews
Pretend You Don't See Her by Mary Higgins Clark
The Q Continuum: Q-Space and Q-Zone by Greg Cox
Clive Cussler and Dirk Pitt Revealed by Clive Cussler
Flood Tide by Clive Cussler
Three Wishes by Barbara Delinsky
An Angel for Emily by Jude Deveraux
Come the Spring by Julie Garwood
Taylor Hanson by Nancy Krulik
Leonardo DiCaprio: A Biography by Nancy Krulik
Hanson by Jill Matthews
Comanche Moon by Larry McMurtry
Zac Hanson by Matt Netter
The End of the Dream by Ann Rule
The Millionaire Next Door by Thomas J. Stanley and William D.
    Danko
The Dominion War, Books 1–4, by John Vornholt and Diane Carey
The Starr Evidence
The Starr Report

~ POCKET BOOKS—HARDCOVER

1988

Spock's World by Diane Duane

1989

A Fighting Spirit: A Championship Season at Notre Dame by Lou
    Holtz with John Heisler
Red Army by Ralph Peters

1990

Under Siege by Stephen Coonts
A Knight in Shining Armor by Jude Deveraux
The Lost Years by J. M. Dillard
The Prime Directive by Judith Reeves-Stevens and Garfield Reeves-
    Stevens

1991

And the Beat Goes On by Sonny Bono
The Duchess by Jude Deveraux
Reunion by Michael Jan Friedman
Paradise by Judith McNaught

1992

Star Trek Probe by Margaret Wander Bonanno
Best Destiny (Star Trek) by Diane L. Carey
Imzadi (Star Trek the Next Generation) by Peter David
Sweet Liar by Jude Deveraux
I Can't Believe I Said That by Kathie Lee Gifford
Keeping the Love You Find by Harville Hendrix
The Way Things Ought to Be by Rush Limbaugh
Rogue Warrior by Richard Marcinko and John Weisman
For Love Alone by Ivana Trump

1993

The Red Horseman by Stephen Coonts
Amy Fisher: My Story by Amy Fisher and Sheila Weller
Keeping the Love You Find by Harville Hendrix
See, I Told You So by Rush Limbaugh
Perfect by Judith McNaught
Rogue Warrior by Richard Marcinko

1994

Sarek by S. C. Crispin

Pocket Books hardcover bestsellers, continued

Q-Squared by Peter David
Star Trek Generations by J. M. Dillard
All Good Things by Michael Jan Friedman
Until You by Judith McNaught
Rogue Warrior II: Red Cell by Richard Marcinko
Star Trek Federation by Judith Reeves-Stevens and Garfield Reeves-Stevens

1995

Intruders by Stephen Coonts
Trust Me by Jayne Ann Krentz

1996

For the Roses by Julie Garwood

1997

The Day After Roswell by Philip Corso
Legend by Jude Deveraux
The Wedding by Julie Garwood
Come the Spring by Julie Garwood
Harvest by Tess Gerritsen
Absolutely, Positively by Jayne Ann Krentz
Deep Waters by Jayne Ann Krentz
Evidence Dismissed by Tom Lange and Philip Vannatter
Remember When by Judith McNaught
Designation Gold by Richard Marcinko and John Weisman
Avenger by William Shatner
Tears of Rage by John Walsh and Susan Schindenette

1998

Now You See Her by Linda Howard
Flash by Jayne Ann Krentz
Sharp Edges by Jayne Ann Krentz
Night Whispers by Judith McNaught

Acknowledgments

THIS HISTORY WOULD NOT HAVE BEEN POSSIBLE without the help of many people. We would like to thank Marcella Berger, Gypsy da Silva, Kate Fischer, Amy Hill, Michael Korda, Annik La Farge, Carolyn Reidy, Jack Romanos, David Rosenthal, Michael Selleck, Judith Trojan, and Irene Yohay.

We are particularly indebted to the anonymously written pamphlet *Simon & Schuster, Our First Fifty Years,* and to Geoffrey Hellman's 1939 three part series on Simon & Schuster in *The New Yorker,* and when memories and back files failed us we consulted Peter Schwed's splendid memoir, *Turning the Pages: An Insider's Story of Simon & Schuster 1924–1984* (Macmillan, 1984).

But above all we wish to thank Wendy Nicholson, Laura Petermann, and Rebecca Rego whose generous gifts of time were what made this project possible.

1: *The Movies.* Griffith & Mayer.
2: Post 1941 through 1980s.
3: Bernard Quint (?). *The Jump Book,* Philippe Halsman, 1959.
4: Charles Addams.
5: Salvador Dali. *Wine, Women, and Words,* Billy Rose.
6: Strome Lamon. Ad for *Very Lovely People,* Ludovic Kennedy, 1970.
7: Paul Coker or Will Hunt. *Pay the Two Dollars,* Alexander Rose, 1957.
8: Circa 1960s.
9: Hilary Knight. *Eloise,* Kay Thompson, 1955.
10: 1930s?
11: Roberta MacDonald. *How to Live with a Cat,* Margaret Cooper Gay, 1946.

156

12: Roberta MacDonald. *How to Live with a Dog,* Margaret Cooper Gay.
13: Siné. *French Cat,* 1958.
14: The original. 1924.
15: Unknown.
16: Circa 1960s.
17: Strome Lamon. Ad for *From Those Wonderful Folks Who Gave You Pearl Harbor,* Jerry Della Femina, 1970.
18: 1930s.
19: 1920s.
20: Strome Lamon. Ad for *The Nashville Sound,* Paul Hemphill, 1970.
21: Circa 1960 through 1986.
22: Circa 1960 through 1986.
23: Daniel Rembert. 1999.
24: Printer's stamp version.
25: Circa 1930 through 1941.
26: Abner Dean.
27: *Slightly Overdrawn,* Thomas L. Stix, ed., 1950.
28: Frankfurt Gips Balkind, 1986.
29: Whitney Darrow, Jr.
30: Used for the "Inner Sanctum" column in *Publishers Weekly* and *The New York Times.*
31: Roger Price, early 1950s.
32: Walt Kelly. *Uncle Pogo So-So Stories,* Walt Kelly, 1953.
33: H. Lawrence Hoffman. Trial design for *The Canterbury Tales,* never used.
34: Paul Smith. *The New Encyclopedia of Modern Bodybuilding,* Arnold Schwarzenegger, 1998.
35: Unknown. 1920s.
36: Amy Hill. *Footnotes,* by Tommy Tune, 1997.
37: Whitney Darrow, Jr.
38: Frederick E. Banbery. *The Pickwick Papers,* special edition (1954?).
39: Tom Funk. *How to Clean Everything,* Alma Chesnut Moore, 1960.
40: George Price.
41: Roy Doty. *The Unfair Sex,* Nina Farewell, 1953.

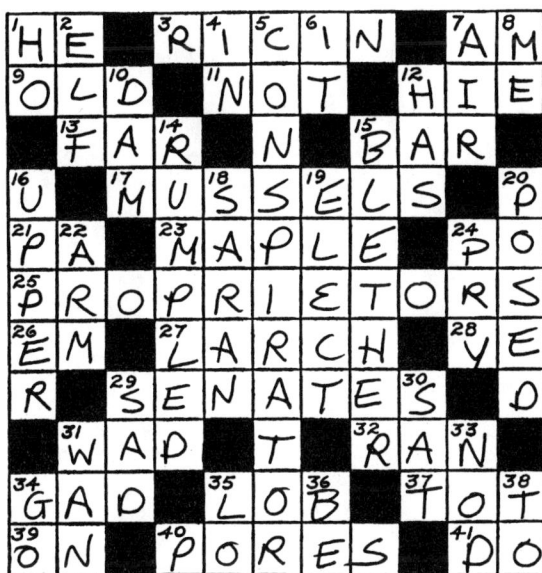

❧ Solution to puzzle on pages 10-11